Generation
CHANGE

Generation
CHANGE

150 Ways We Can Change Ourselves, Our Country, and Our World

Jayan Kalathil and Melissa Bolton-Klinger

Skyhorse Publishing

Skyhorse Publishing books may be purchased in bulk at special discounts for sales promotion, corporate gifts, fund-raising, or educational purposes. Special editions can also be created to specifications. For details, contact the Special Sales Department, Skyhorse Publishing, 555 Eighth Avenue, Suite 903, New York, NY 10018 or info@skyhorsepublishing.com.

www.skyhorsepublishing.com

10 9 8 7 6 5 4 3 2 1

Library of Congress Cataloging-in-Publication Data

Bolton-Klinger, Melissa, Kalathil, Jayan.
Generation change : 150 ways we can change ourselves, our country, and our world / Jayan Kalathil and Melissa Bolton-Klinger.
p. cm.
ISBN 978-1-60239-730-9
1. Social participation—United States. 2. Social change—United States. 3. Youth—United States—Attitides. 4. Self-actualization (Psychology) I. Bolton-Klinger, Melissa. II. Title.
HN59.2.K345 2009
303.48'409051—dc22
2009026075

Printed in the United States of America

"Change will not come if we wait for some other person or some other time. We are the ones we've been waiting for. We are the change that we seek."

—President Barack Obama (February 5, 2008)

CONTENTS

Section II
Change Our Country

Chapter 4: The House of You

Section III
Change Our World

INTRODUCTION

66

"Every so often, there are times when America must rise to meet a moment. So it has been for the generation that built the railroads and beat back the Depression; that worked on the first assembly line and that went to the moon. So it must be for us today. This is our moment. This is our time to unite in common purpose, to make this century the next American century. Because when Americans come together, there is no destiny too difficult or too distant for us to reach."
—President Barack Obama (June 16, 2008)

99

On November 4, 2008, the world entered a new era as Barack Obama was elected the forty-fourth president of the United States of America. With this momentous occasion, a new generation of foot soldiers was mobilized, ready to work for and with the man who rallied a nation with his now memorable campaign slogan, "Yes we can!" The largest demo in the United States is armed to the teeth with tech savvy and fearless optimism. "Generation Change" is ready to change the world. And that means you!

This is no ordinary presidency, people. That much was clear from the start. Even before he officially announced that he was running for the office of president of the United States, the former junior senator from Illinois seemed to possess an uncanny ability to unite people of all ages, races, religions, and political backgrounds. And in the end, they came together during his campaign to elect a man who represented all that might be possible for America's future. The rich, the poor, the young, the old, the gay, the straight, the liberal, and the conservative alike all seemed to feel that Barack Obama was the person that best spoke for their vision of the country. His message particularly seemed to ring true among the 30-and-under set, who finally saw a person who was speaking for them. After years of feeling sidelined by the political process, many young Americans rallied to his side perhaps because they saw a person with whom they could finally relate. A person who was just as comfortable rubbing elbows with world leaders as he was rubbing elbows with Jay-Z and Beyoncé. A person who at one moment could be picking the men and women for his cabinet, and the next be picking his bracket for the NCAA basketball tourney. A person who carried a BlackBerry, who knew what *Gossip Girl* was, and who not so long ago was just another young person with big dreams of changing the world—a person like you!

But the job doesn't stop now that he's in office. In fact, now is when the work really begins. We put the man in charge, but now it's time for us to get down to business. In the following pages you'll find a variety of different ideas—some big, some small—of what you can do to create change for yourself, your country, and your world. Some were inspired by our president, some were inspired by people around us, and some we just came up with on our own. We try to present each in a very simple way with a few tips for you to take to heart, and peppered throughout we've added quotes from the president to keep you inspired. We also provide various organizations, Web sites, books, television shows, and films for you to look into on your own and to get you thinking. They're a mix of both serious and light-hearted suggestions for you to explore, and hopefully you'll discover something new about different causes, different organizations, different people, and different ideas. But the best ideas probably won't come from this book. They'll come from you. This is just the jumping-off point. Where you go from here is wide open.

So turn the page, take a deep breath, and get ready to jump in!

—Jayan and Melissa

"What is required of us now is a new era of responsibility, a recognition, on the part of every American, that we have duties to ourselves, our nation, and the world, duties that we do not grudgingly accept but rather seize gladly, firm in the knowledge that there is nothing so satisfying to the spirit, so defining of our character, than giving our all to a difficult task."

—President Barack Obama (January 20, 2009)

1. Read President Obama's Books

Hey, Generation Change, we're glad you're here. Hopefully you'll be interested in some of the ideas we've written down in the following pages. But before you dive in, take a moment to learn more about the leader of Generation Change. In other words, while we all obviously know who President Obama is, do you know his life story and where he stands on certain issues? If your answer is "ummm . . . ," allow us to give you the first tip of our book. Pick up the three books you should read to get a better perspective on our president.

The first is *Dreams from My Father*, a book he wrote when he was just finishing law school. This book was not written by Barack Obama the politician. It was written by Barack Obama the young man with a life full of promise ahead of him, but who was still struggling with his own past and where he was going. It's open and heartfelt, and you get an honest look into the heart and mind of the man in the Oval Office. The next book is *The Audacity of Hope*, written by the president when he was still a junior senator from Illinois. In it, he outlines his views on politics, race, faith, family, America, and the world. When you read this book, you can tell that although he is still a rookie politician, he has a twinkle in his eye that hints at something greater. The last book is *Change We Can Believe In*. Published during his presidential campaign, this book outlines his vision for what he wants for America. While he is not the author of this book, it does contain a foreword that he wrote and several of his key campaign speeches. This book is a great tool to use to see where he stands on major issues and what he campaigned for. So go on, put this book down, and pick up those three. We're serious! We won't get offended, and we'll be here for ya when you get back. Promise!

READ

Dreams from My Father by Barack Obama
The Audacity of Hope by Barack Obama
Change We Can Believe In by Obama for America

Generation
CHANGE

SECTION I
Change Ourselves

Change usually comes from within. So where better to start off than by changing ourselves? We know, we know, we think you're pretty perfect too! But we can always improve and add on a little to perfection, right? Besides, these changes are fun (not like a root canal or anything) and they are 99 percent guaranteed to make you a better you. Why only 99 percent? Well, we had to give ourselves an out just in case, right? We're not licensed therapists after all. Think of these ideas as a mini self-improvement course before you head off to save the world. Because that's why you're reading this book after all, right? We thought so.

CHAPTER 1

MIND

2. Put Down the Remote and Pick Up a Book

"Replace the video game or remote control with a book once in a while."
—President Barack Obama (June 15, 2008)

Technology is great! We love our TiVo and our Playstation as much as the next person. Yeah, we know that watching

The Hills can be addictive, and we get hooked for hours playing *Call of Duty*, too. But there's something to be said about turning off the TV and game console and picking up a book once in a while. If you have to, just consider it exercise (mental exercise, that is) and you don't even need to work up a sweat. And a note to the fellas: nothing impresses the ladies quite like a man who knows his literature, whereas *Grand Theft Auto* secrets . . . hmm, not so much. Reading can be such an escape from the day-to-day drudgery of life, and a great engaging book can offer a much more textualized and expansive world than any video game or movie ever can. Even though we love Peter Jackson's *Lord of the Rings* film trilogy (we even own the extended DVD set), they still can't compare to Tolkien's original written masterpieces. If you don't like "working out" alone, join or start a book club where you can discuss what you read with friends. And if you really can't deal with life without technology, pick up a Kindle and read an e-book. So run out to your local bookstore and check out what's hot on the bestseller list. Just *read something*.

 VISIT

www.gutenberg.org (where you can find free downloads of tons of must-read classics)

> **www.shelfari.com**
>
> **www.weread.com** (where you can join an online community with all the other bookworms of the world)

3. Don't Let the Media Tell You What You're Worth

Hey, Generation Change, we're the most plugged-in generation in history. It's never been easier to get info, connect with each other, and stay up-to-date with the latest trends. We can Google, Facebook, or Tweet to our hearts' content while we watch, read, or listen to things from almost anywhere and while doing almost anything. Being media savvy is great, but there can be too much of a good thing. When we get bombarded left and right about what we should be buying, what we should be wearing, or what we should look like, we can start to doubt ourselves. We might feel too fat, too thin, too poor, too old, or fill-in-whatever-your-own-insecurity-is-here. Advertisers feature models that 99.99 percent of us don't look like, and it's causing a lot of us to have some serious issues ranging from depression and low self-esteem to body image issues and eating disorders. Well, don't believe the hype. Nobody really has skin that smooth or a stomach that toned. It's called Photoshop, people, and if you shell out some dough for a copy for your computer, you too can look that good with a couple of clicks of the mouse. The media is a business based on looks and appearances, but remember that appearances can be deceiving. So don't believe everything that you hear, read, or see. It'll do you good. And if it makes you feel any better, you should know that even the .01 percent of us who are models still break out in acne too.

VISIT

www.about-face.org

4. Create Your Personal Brand

Talk to any marketing professional and they'll tell you that a strong brand is the key to success. Sure, that might make sense in business school, but what does that mean in the real world? And what's a personal brand? Well, like any good company or product, people are brands, too. With the world's economy turned on its head, and more and more people facing layoffs, it's never been more important than now to understand what your personal brand is. So, what is it? Well in a nutshell, it's you. It's all your personality traits, your goals, how you present yourself in different situations, and what people think of when they think of you. We all know people with infectious personalities—people whom we instantly want to get to know better. Well, they've mastered their personal brands and they know how to market themselves in a way that attracts others. And knowing how others perceive you, and how you perceive yourself, is the key to success in any arena. With a strong personal brand, doors open left and right. Dating? No problem. Jobs and career? No problem. Because when you know who you are, what you want, and you are confident about it, there's nothing more attractive. Just look at our president. He exudes confidence every time he speaks because he has a strong sense of self, which is part of the reason why so many people are drawn to him. So follow his example and use your own strengths to get ahead in your life. Set yourself apart and be memorable. Consider these starting points:

- Play to your strengths. Figure out what you're naturally good at and make that work for you.
- Consider doing a 360-degree feedback assessment of your friends, family, coworkers, and classmates to see how everyone perceives you in your life.
- Craft a vision statement for yourself. What is it that you want to represent and stand for?
- Come up with an elevator pitch (a 20-second summary) for both your professional and personal life. You never get a second chance to make a first impression, so make sure you're prepared for any situation.
- Take a personal branding class or seminar to get more specific tips on how to market and sell yourself.

Ultimately you're the CEO of company YOU, so learn to market it properly. And in this company, you're always corner office material!

 VISIT

www.personalbrandingblog.com
www.reachcc.com (offers 360-degree assessments)

READ

StrengthFinders 2.0 by Tom Rath

5. Blah-Blah-Blah Blog for Good

> "The truth is, actually, words do inspire. Words do help people get involved. . . . Don't discount that power."
> —President Barack Obama (January 5, 2008)

Here in America, we've been blessed with the right to free speech. So we say it's time to start using it! And by using it, we mean something beyond status updates telling the world what you ate for lunch that day. Sharing every single little detail all about you is awesome, don't get us wrong, but sometimes all that talk about you, you, you can get a little . . . how do we say this nicely? *Ahem*, boring. Why not turn your words into the powerful tools that they are and start blogging for change? Find that cause that keeps you up at night and get blogging! And we all know the best thing about the blah blah blah blog is that there's no one there to argue with you. Well, that is until the comments start rolling in . . .

Once you get your world-changing blog up and running, make sure to check out Changeblogger (**www.changeblogger.com**) It's the place to connect with others who are blogging, podcasting, and vlogging to make the world a better place.

Need inspiration? Check out *GOOD* magazine's blogs, which range in every topic from Darfur to saving polar bears. What? You haven't heard of *GOOD*? *GOOD* is a magazine that highlights issues and is geared toward people who believe in social activism. Sound like anyone you know? We say run, don't walk!

And if you still don't know how to make a blog, welcome to the "Internets!" It's as easy as one-two-three these days thanks to tons of programs. Our favorites, Tumblr and WordPress, both have apps so you can blog on the go on your iPhone. Get out there and start talking.

 VISIT

www.changeblogger.ning.com
www.good.is
www.tumblr.com
www.wordpress.org

6. Learn How to Debate

Since we've been doing all this talking about talking, why not take it really old school and learn the art of debate? How kick-ass would it be to be able to indisputably prove that global warming does exist to your great aunt in Texas who still believes that we solved that problem in the '80s when we stopped using aerosol hairspray? The beauty of debate is that it allows you to talk about controversial topics, normally considered taboo in social situations, from all sides of the issue. Debate makes no room for finger-pointing. Rather, it encourages looking at a topic from different angles and viewpoints in a more calm and collected manner, which ultimately makes for a less hotheaded discussion. Let's face it: There are facts to back up every opinion but by learning the basic rules of debate you can ensure that your point comes across as logical and approachable, both of which are surefire ways to bring someone closer to accepting your point of view.

Try these tips on for size to get you started:

- First off, you need to do some research. You're going to need some facts to back up your statements.
- Remember to have an open mind. You may find yourself thinking what the other person is saying sounds

like something you *could* believe in. It's okay to change your opinion.

- Try to think of the other side of the argument as well as your side. There's a reason we all have different opinions. The more you know about why someone believes in something, the better prepared you'll be to have solid facts to show why they should see things your way.
- Don't stray off of the subject. Always keep to the topic at hand.
- Don't be mean or attack the other person below the belt. Debating should be fun, and all finger-pointing should be left at home.

The time is now to put an end to heated shouting matches that never end in anything other than anger and start using some good old-fashioned debating skills. Feel free to buy yourself a shrunken blazer with a school crest and start a local debate club when you're done brushing up on the basics.

 VISIT

www.yourdebate.net/tips.asp (for more tips and tricks)

WATCH

The film *Rocket Science* (2007) directed by Jeffrey Blitz

7. Use Twitter and Instant Messaging for Good

While we're talking about words, let's not forget our 140-character friends over there at Twitter and our indispensable mode of quick conversation, IM. The great thing about Twitter, texting, and IM is that they're all immediate, which is great when you're trying to get people's attention. Making things more bite-sized makes it easier to get people to really notice what you're saying.

So nxt time U wnt 2 tell all 13,409 of yr friends abt the daily injustices happening 2 Polar Bears in the Arctic, try Tweeting. Short is not only sweet—it can be incredibly world changing as well.

Need help converting your monologues into something smaller? Try **tweetshrink.com** or **twonvert.com**, which will instantly make your words more Twitter friendly.

IM can save the world! The i'm Initiative from Microsoft makes helping social causes easy. Every time you use Windows Live Messenger or Windows Live Hotmail, they'll share a portion of their advertising revenue with the cause you choose from a list including UNICEF, **stopglobalwarming.org**, and the Humane Society. Kinda makes the "PC" in those Apple commercials seem pretty cool now too.

Hey, don't forget about your old trusted friend, e-mail. By signing up for **replyforall.com**, you will automatically see the cause of your choice in your messages. The more messages you send, the more money goes to your cause—courtesy of sponsors. The more of you who join, the more the sponsors pay, and then the more the causes receive! Whew. Money for your cause just by e-mailing party pics to your friend across the country? Sign us up!

Need some inspiration? Check out these game-changing Twitter users:

- See the man at work at **www.twitter.com /BarackObama**
- See how others have been using Twitter for good! **www.twestival.com**
- For fun just! Like Yoda, try Twittering! That make you sound, how wise will, hmm? *Herh herh herh.* **www.yodaspeak.co.uk**

VISIT

www.tweetshrink.com
www.twonvert.com
www.im.live.com
www.replyforall.com
www.twitter.com/BarackObama
www.twestival.com
www.yodaspeak.co.uk

8. Know Your American History and Herstory

America has one of the most interesting histories of all the countries in the world. Of course we're the first to admit that we're totally biased, but given the relatively young age of our nation, it's pretty cool what we've been able to accomplish in such a short period of time. Our country's history is filled with amazing stories from the Revolutionary War to the fables of how the West was won to the election of our current president. So do you know our story? Obviously it's impossible to know everything there is to know about American history since history encapsulates the entire human condition. But the more you learn, the more you can see how everything, and everyone, is interconnected. It shows us how and why the world around us is structured as we see it, and when you look at life in a grander scheme rather than just separate isolated events and incidents, you see how one thing runs into the next, and how everything eventually affects everything else.

For example, the bombing of Pearl Harbor led to America's involvement in WWII, which ended with America becoming a world superpower along with the USSR. This kicked off the Cold War, and it was during the Cold War that Osama bin Laden was trained in Afghanistan. And unfortunately as we all know, this eventually led to the tragic events of 9/11.

The more you know about our history, the more you can understand both the how and the why that things happen, and the smarter and more informed and well rounded you'll be. We'll leave it up to you to decide what aspect of American history you're into, from the Pilgrims at Plymouth to those radical '60s, the Great Depression or the modern-day recession, the choices are limitless. But it's a good thing to know more and dig deeper than just what you learned in high school. Remember, there are always two sides to every story, and the textbook history we learn in school is usually written from the victor's perspective. So try to look at things from both sides to get the full picture of what really happened.

VISIT

www.history.com

READ

A People's History of the United States by Howard Zinn
America by Jon Stewart (if you want a comical POV)

WATCH

The History Channel
The films *Flags of Our Fathers* (2006) and *Letters from Iwo Jima* (2006) directed by Clint Eastwood

9. Just Say No to Slactivism

Don't be a slactivist! Go beyond the Facebook badge and take some time to really learn about those causes you've been "supporting." It's great to have something to believe in, and by aligning yourself with a cause, you're helping them with the most important part of their mission: heightening awareness. Now take the next step and do some research and learn more about their programs. Find out not just what they stand for, but the specifics of the programs they've created too. Or the origins of the organization, like when they got started and why. Even better, learn statistics associated with the cause so you can talk about it with confidence when you go home for Thanksgiving. You're their wo/man on the street after all, and you need to be armed with all the pertinent info so you can spread the word to everyone you meet. Still don't know what you should be championing? Read the paper or walk around your neighborhood and see what issue gets your blood boiling. And don't forget to check out **change.org** or *GOOD* magazine's Web site where they outline a ton of pressing issues that are sure to get your heart racing better than a round of Tae Bo.

 VISIT

www.good.is
www.change.org

10. Know the News

While print newspapers and magazines might be dropping like flies these days, the news is never going to die. It's easier than ever to get all kinds of news about any subject you want. So whether you read the *New York Times* or the *Washington Post*, watch CNN or Fox News, read Google or Yahoo!, or follow any of the countless blogs or Tweets online. What's important is that you stay up-to-date with what's going on in the world around you. It's never been easier to get instant access to the latest headlines from around the world, and with today's cell phones and PDAs, you don't even need to be near a computer anymore. Sure, we can try to bury our heads in the sand and not worry about the world outside our little life bubbles. But the events of the past 10 years should be proof enough to everyone that we all need to know what's going on around us. The world is only going to keep getting smaller and smaller as technology improves, and we will all become more and more interconnected. Americans will need to keep up, know what's going on, and continue to lead. And that means being smarter, more versatile, and better informed. So give yourself at least 15 minutes every day to catch up on the headlines. If anything, think of this time spent as an investment for your conversations at your next cocktail party.

11. Be a Lifelong Learner

"With the changing economy, no one has lifetime employment. But community colleges provide lifetime employability."
—President Barack Obama (February 19, 2005)

President Obama has made it quite clear that he believes getting an education is of the utmost importance, and we couldn't agree more. If you haven't graduated from high school, you should consider getting your GED or attending a two-year community college and getting a degree in something you've been interested in but haven't known how to pursue. And just because you already have that degree in hand doesn't mean the learning should stop there. Practice the idea of becoming a lifelong learner, which is very easy.

Studies have proven that the brain needs to be constantly stimulated, so why not get online and sign up for that class in computer programming and wow your friends with how much you know about Linux?

More of the study-at-your-own-pace type? Download textbooks on any subject you can imagine at **ibiblio.org**. Best thing is, it's free. And electronic! Feel free to read out loud here—this library is in your house after all.

Ever wanted to say you graduated from MIT? Well now you can. According to the MIT Web site, "MIT OpenCourseWare (OCW) is a web-based publication of virtually all MIT course content. OCW is open and available to the world and is a permanent MIT activity." So get ready to do some learning, because you're going back to college. Damn, it feels good to have a big brain.

VISIT

www.mit.edu
www.ibiblio.org

12. Think Before You Speak

Ever stick your foot in your mouth? No, not literally, as we can't all be yoga experts, but figuratively. Of course you have, who hasn't? It happens to the best of us; we hear or see something that really pisses us off and we go off the deep end and rip into someone face to face, leave a nasty voicemail, or fire off an angry e-mail or text. Well these days things get even more complicated because with technology, once you send something into the depths of cyberspace, it's not easy to take it back. Sometimes being a hothead is something that we can't always control, and it can lead to many situations where we open mouth and insert foot. Many a relationship and professional reputation have been damaged and destroyed because people didn't wait a beat to calm down before they reacted. The next time this happens to you, take a moment to pause before you respond. Consider these suggestions:

- Step back from the situation and take a deep breath to try to relax your body.
- Repeat a calming word, like "relax" or "woosa" while gently massaging your earlobes with your thumb and forefinger.
- Visualize a peaceful or relaxing experience from your past until you've calmed down.

It may sound silly, but we've found that when we feel like we're about to explode, we take a break to get over it and wait a few to think things over so we're able to respond in a way that doesn't leave egg on our face later on.

VISIT

www.angermgmt.com
www.angermanagementtips.com
www.apa.org/topics/controlanger.html

13. Protest Peacefully

Some things in life just piss us off. Like when our Netflix DVDs show up scratched, but usually we get over that in a few hours. But there are other things that we can't get over so easily. We're talking about the big things in life that really get stuck in our craw. You know, things that the government or corporations may do that make us so upset that we just wanna punch a wall. Well, that's usually not the best approach. In fact, it'll probably just make things worse (and break our hands in the process). But this is America, people, and we're allowed to show and voice our dissatisfaction peacefully. People are literally dying in other parts of the world because they can't protest, so be thankful for this right and take advantage of it! Whatever you feel passionately about, get out there, get together, get organized, and let your voice be heard. But remember the key word is *peacefully*. Don't be breaking any windows or throwing any Molotov cocktails on our watch! Strange as it is, you're likely to get a lot further singing "Kumbaya" over and over than if you were throwing stones. History is filled with examples that illustrate this. Our country's most famous is Martin Luther King Jr., of course, but he took his cue from Mahatma Gandhi. Both of them were successful because they organized to protest for causes that they felt were just. So whatever it is that's getting you hot under the collar, don't just take it. Take some action instead. Start or sign a petition, create a group on an online social network, join a campaign, stage a sit-in, hold a walkout, attend a rally or a vigil, organize a march, plan a boycott. There are countless ways to make your voice heard. Whatever your cause is, go shout it from the rooftops and find some like-minded people. The only way that you will ever get anything done is by getting people organized, so start organizing! And by the way, do you know what one of the president's first jobs was? Community organizer. Nuff said. Check out the following to get you inspired while you paint those picket signs.

WATCH

The film *Gandhi* (1982) starring Sir Ben Kingsey

READ

Civil Disobedience by Henry David Thoreau

14. Don't Tolerate Prejudice

> "The walls between races and tribes; natives and immigrants; Christian and Muslim and Jew cannot stand. These now are the walls we must tear down."
> —President Barack Obama (July 24, 2008)

Okay, truth be told, we're all prejudiced. C'mon, be honest and cut the political correctness for a second. Each of us harbors some sort of unspoken prejudice, even if we don't admit it. Us? Well, we simply can't stand guys who wear shorts and dress shoes with colored socks pulled up to their knees. There, we admitted it! But if you can acknowledge your own prejudices, then you've taken a first step toward dealing with the issue. When people don't keep their prejudiced views to themselves it's an opportunity to speak up. We've all been there: a friend tells a racist joke or makes a sexist or homophobic remark and we don't say anything, even if we're uncomfortable with it. So next time, don't just shrug. If your friends say something out of line, call them on it. Hey, at least you'll know you did the right thing. And if you can, take a visit to the Museum of Tolerance in Los Angeles for a first-hand look at the issue of prejudice and intolerance.

 VISIT

www.understandingprejudice.org
www.museumoftolerance.com

 WATCH

The film *American History X* (1998) starring Edward Norton

READ

To Kill A Mockingbird by Harper Lee

15. Make a Buzzworthy Public Service Announcement on the Web

Come on, Generation Change, the world is watching. What do you have to say? Sure, making a video about kicking your brother in the balls is funny, but why don't you do something more positive with YouTube? Today there is no tool more powerful than the Internet to get your message out there and a video can't go viral until it's made. First things first: Choose a cause you believe in, then get your camera and start shooting.

Tips for a good Internet PSA:

1. Less is more. Not that we don't think you have tons to say, but with the excessive amount of content out there, you need to cut to the chase and make your message stand out. Aim to make something under

two minutes, because let's face it, we all have a short attention spans these days.

2. Don't forget about audio. A picture may be worth a thousand words, but good sound is priceless. If you don't already have one, invest in an external microphone for your handy cam. Trust us, it makes all the difference in the world.

3. Edit. Edit. Edit. And if you have doubts, see tip number one. Martin Scorsese might be able to pull off kick-ass one-shots, but for the rest of us, don't forget the power of editing. If you can, use Final Cut Pro or iMovie to make your PSA more memorable.

4. Casting is key. Sure your BFF is free, but there are a ton of actors out there looking to work on a good project. If your PSA is scripted, try placing an ad on Craigslist or start trolling your Facebook friends' pages for someone to make your PSA feel more professional.

5. Buy a beret. You're the director after all.

 VISIT

www.youthnoise.com (a site where you can join or start causes and network with others who have shared beliefs)

hub.witness.org (the global platform for human rights media and action and a pro-social alternative to YouTube)

 READ

Film Directing: Shot by Shot: Visualizing from Concept to Screen by Steven Katz (Start thinking like a director. This book is a good crash course in Film-making 101.)

16. Communicate Beyond Emoticons

If we've learned anything from President Obama, it's that there's nothing more powerful or inspiring than a mastery of words and the ability to captivate and mobilize people. He made talking to 500,000 people look so easy and effortless. Where were the sweaty palms? Or the "ummms" or "ahhhs"? And even post election during his first few months as president, he addressed the nation time after time speaking to difficult topics with a seemingly absence of worry or fear. "How does he do it?" you may ask. Well, it looks like he has what we call a mastery of public speaking. Sure most of us had to take the requisite public speaking class in high school or college where we fumbled through a five-minute word fest about some seemingly inconsequential topic, but when was the last time we brushed off those public speaking skills and spoke to a group? Probably not recently, as many of our jobs don't involve addressing the free world on a daily basis. But that doesn't mean we shouldn't all know how to speak in front of a crowd. Even if you're in a meeting and you have to present a project to five people, you'll be surprised at how much more effective it will be if you learn to captivate your audience in a calm and clear manner. So why don't you take some time and learn how to speak in public? Your next meeting will thank you.

Here are a few tips that should get you up and speaking in public in no time:

- You should know what you're talking about. Do your research and have a basic understanding of what you're saying. Even if that means scanning Wikipedia (our trusty Internet version of CliffsNotes). Trust us, the more info you have, the better.
- Check out the space you'll be speaking in before you have to actually make the speech or presentation. That way you'll know what the acoustics and the lighting

are like. No surprises will ensure you'll be calmer and better able to concentrate on what you're saying.

- Like everything in life, practice, practice, practice makes perfect! Even if that means going over your speech with your cat, your plant, or your best friend fifty times before the real deal, the more times you actually do your speech, the better it will be for the actual event.

- Have confidence—or fake it till you make it. Be like the president and seem calm, cool, and collected even if you're not. Try taking deep breaths if you start to feel flustered. And slow down. Chances are if you're nervous, you'll start talking faster—a big giveaway that you've got the jitters. Slower is always better in speech making.

- Loosen up. You need to be fluid. Try using hand gestures and facial expressions while you're talking. No one wants to listen to an automaton.

- Try not to read while looking down. Make eye contact with the crowd. Scan the room for different people to connect with, and shift your gaze often. This will make people feel like you're talking *with* them, rather than *at* them.

Now get on that stage of life and start talking. We can't wait to hear what you have to say!

VISIT

www.toastmasters.org (for more tips and tricks)
www.obamaspeeches.com (to get inspired by the master)

READ

The Art of Public Speaking by Dale Carnegie

17. Turn Off Technology

Put the BlackBerry down. Turn off TiVo. Tell the computer to take a break. Just say no to anything that has a screen, buttons, or knobs. In other words, it's time to unplug from all that technology that fills our daily lives and stop to smell the flowers of life. When was the last time you sat in silence or stopped to think about what is important to you rather than being told what everyone else is thinking about? We love technology more than words can even say, but we also appreciate the simpler things that don't require electricity. It not only saves the planet, but it also saves your brain cells from information overload. Take a class, watch the stars, talk to a friend. It doesn't matter what you do, as long as it doesn't have a battery. Become a neo-luddite. Try it. You might like it.

18. Protect Your (Online) Rep

Twenty years ago, most people didn't know what e-mail was. Fifteen years ago, the Web was barely getting off the ground. And ten years ago, no one had a MySpace or Facebook page. How quickly the times change. But we Americans are a clever and resourceful bunch, so we readily adapt to any technology that Silicon Valley throws our way. These days, we're living our lives online for all the world to see, blogging our hearts out, Tweeting till we're out of breath, and updating our status every ten seconds. We're networking and poaching friends and friends of friends that we haven't seen in years, and learning all about their lives without even having to talk to them. Kinda weird, actually. But maybe we should be a bit cautious about what we put out there in cyberland and who we're connecting with online. Remember that picture of you doing that keg stand over the weekend? Awesome dude, but probably not the best one to post when your mom is online too. And that status update of how hungover you are today after calling in sick to work yesterday? Hmm . . . sometimes bosses and coworkers are on social networks too. And every post you write on your page or someone else's page? Yeah, that's all logged and stored somewhere on some giant central servers, and it never goes away once it's out there. Keep that in mind the next time you are interviewing for a job, or applying to a school, or dating that new guy or gal, because all it takes is a Web-savvy person with a search engine and some time to kill to dig up all kinds of online dirt. Here are a couple tips to consider:

- Keep any pics of you totally wasted offline. And pics of you naked. That's just common sense.
- Be careful of who you talk smack about in postings. It's not always the best idea to broadcast that to the world. If you really have to, keep it limited to text messages or e-mails.
- Think twice about joining a group on a social networking site with a name like "I like to get drunk and naked and take pictures with random strangers." Even if you do like to do that, might be best to keep that to yourself because it'll show up in your profile.

- Finally, if you absolutely can't help yourself, then at least make sure to control your privacy settings! If you really feel the need to share everything in your life with everyone you've ever known and met, then please share it with only those people that can't fire or hire you in the future.

Your rep is your rep, whether it's online or not. So protect it!

 VISIT

www.onlinereputation.com (for some interesting posts on this subject)

19. Be a Risk Taker

"It has been the risk takers, the doers, the makers of things—some celebrated, but more often men and women obscure in their labor—who have carried us up the long, rugged path toward prosperity and freedom."

—President Barack Obama (January 20, 2009)

Do you like to play it safe? You know, rather than going after what you want in life, do you just sit back and hope that things will come to you? Do you take the main path rather than the road less traveled? If so, then congratulations! You've just earned yourself a lifetime of boredom! Sorry, not to get harsh on you guys, but life is all about taking risks. Whether it's gathering up the nerve to ask that special someone out on a first date or heading into the corner office to state your case about why you deserve that promotion, in both cases, you gotta put yourself out there. Sure it's scary sometimes, but it's the only way to ever get anywhere worthwhile in life. Besides, who wants a boring, mundane existence anyway? Now whether or not you want to take up BASE jumping or swimming with sharks is up to you. There's something to be said about putting yourself on the line from time to time. Don't over-think things, or you'll just end up psyching yourself out more than you need to. And keep Nike's old slogan in mind and "just do it." Sometimes things work out, sometimes they don't, but at least in the back of your head you'll know that you tried, because there's nothing worse than the nagging feeling of regret. Unless it's the feeling of knowing that your parachute isn't opening, but that's the reason why we don't go BASE jumping in the first place.

Kidding. So the moral of this story, kids, is that in life, you gotta have some balls. And if you don't have any, well, you best start growing a pair.

CHAPTER 2

BODY

20. Laugh and Smile More

Just say no to drugs—except the natural ones! A recent study at the University of Maryland suggested that laughing and smiling not only helps lower your blood pressure, but releases endorphins and serotonin as well. But wait, there's more! They also found that a good har, har, har can help reduce stress, elevate your mood, boost your immune system, improve brain function, and protect your heart. Sounds like the doctor ordered a heavy dose of turn-that-frown-upside-down. So what're you waiting for? Start smilin'!

Need something to make you smile?

 VISIT

www.ajokeaday.com
www.funnyordie.com
www.icanhascheezburger.com
www.sleeveface.com
www.theonion.com

 WATCH

The "Christian the Lion" clip on YouTube (for a guaranteed smile and an "awww" to go with it)

21. Take a Food Adventure

Another turkey sandwich for lunch again? And the same old pasta for dinner too, huh? BOR-RING! Sounds like you need to go on a food adventure! Don't get us wrong, we love our pizza, burgers, and mac 'n' cheese as much as the next person, but there's a world of culinary delights waiting for you if you just broaden your food horizons. It's a lot of fun to try new ethnic foods, and you may just become hooked. Never had Shanghainese soup dumplings before? What about Vietnamese banh mi sandwiches? Or Venezuelan arepas or Argentinian empanadas? Spanish tapas? Middle Eastern shawarma? Italian gelato? Mexican fish tacos? Indian masala dosas? If not, then you are missing the fun and it's time for you to try branching out. Take a look online or in your local phone book and check out all the different types of ethnic or alternative restaurants that are nearby and that aren't your normal fare. Then get on out there and start eating! Trust us, you never knew so many strange-sounding dishes could taste so delicious. If you want to play it safe, ask the waiter what the popular dishes are or what the chef recommends, and get ready to get your grub on. Not only will you feel incredibly full and satisfied afterward, chances are you'll also gain a better appreciation for different cultures as well. So eat up, kids!

WATCH

The show *No Reservations* on the Travel Channel
The Food Network

22. Say Bye-Bye to Bad Habits

Okay, okay. We're sure you're tired of hearing this one, but you are what you eat, drink, and put into your body. Let's be honest, it's time to put down those cigarettes (that includes you Mr. President). Say goodbye to all those bad habits in your life and replace them with really good ones. We'll stop preaching now. (But seriously, we're watching you, Mr. President. Nicorette called and they want to give you your healthy lungs back.)

 VISIT

www.wikihow.com/Break-a-Habit
www.43things.com (Get people to cheer you on as you try to break your habit at this online goal-setting community. Because we all know everything hard in life is easier to accomplish with the help of others!)

23. Obamafy Yourself

The artist Shepard Fairey's iconic poster of President Obama was pretty much everywhere during the game-changing election. You know the one, where a graphic version of him was looking off into the distance with the word "hope" loud and proud beneath him. Now it's your turn to look just like the president! All you have to do is upload a photo and you too can be more like Barack thanks to some clever software designers roaming the World Wide Web. And when you're done, join all the other B'Rock wannabes and post the new Obamafied version of yourself on Flickr. Just go to Flickr and type in "Obamafy."

 VISIT

www.dubster.com/obamafy
www.flickr.com

24. Get Your Heart Pumping

Let's face the facts: Humans are meant to be active creatures, not just couch potatoes. Yeah, we know it's fun to veg out and watch the game all day long, but wouldn't it be more fun if you were out there actually *playing* the game? And we don't mean playing it on your Xbox. We mean doing something that actually gets your heart pumping. So get out there and start being active! Go for a walk, ride a bike, take a swim, surf, jog, play some ball, go rock climbing, go snowboarding, practice yoga, just get out there and go. Listen, we know that not everyone loves exercising when it means going to the gym and running in place or lifting weights for hours on end. We feel ya. You don't need six-pack abs to let you know you're getting in shape. As long as we stay active, in whatever form that we choose that seems fun, and watch what we eat, we're all going to start getting healthier. And America needs to get healthier. Plus it's never been more fun to work out than with today's gym classes, DVDs for your home, and portable music to keep you motivated. Even the president plays ball to stay in shape. So record that game on your DVR, put down that remote and video game controller, and get moving, people!

VISIT

www.presidentschallenge.org
www.fitnessonline.com

 WATCH

The reality show *The Biggest Loser*

---

25. Live a Little

Life is for the taking! Who ever said we're supposed to be corporate drones that live to work rather than work to live? Okay, yeah we all gotta make a paycheck, but don't forget that our lives outside of work matter too. So get out there and enjoy it. We're serious—if you don't grab life by the horns now, you're gonna regret it fifty years from now when your back goes out. Listen, no one on his or her deathbed ever says, "I really wish I had spent more time in the office." Nah, it's more like, "Damnit, I wish I'd gone skydiving!" Go bungee jumping, summit a mountain, ride a scary roller coaster, go white water rafting, take an adventure trip, do anything that gets the blood pumping and adrenaline going, because that's when you know you're alive. And we like a little debauchery, too (within reason people), so it's great to get a little crazy once in a while. Put a pub crawl together with your BFFs, do sake bombs while you wail your heart out at a karaoke bar, play some slosh-ball with your friends in the park. Laugh, smile, and enjoy life with the ones you love. Hey, isn't that the whole point of living? Check out the following links for some ideas on how to have some fun and adventure. Party on!

 VISIT

www.globaladrenaline.com (for you adventure trip junkies)

www.incredible-adventures.com (for mind-blowing adrenaline rushes)

www.santacon.com (for some Christmastime debauchery and cheer)

www.snuggiepubcrawls.com (for some good old fashioned drunken fun)

26. Watch What You Eat

Okay, we know you've heard this one before, but we have a serious problem on our hands and it's time we stop the madness. America is getting fat! The fact is, America's waistline is expanding and it doesn't look like it's going to stop anytime soon. And while a lot of it has to do with the fact that we're not exercising enough, it also has to do with what we're putting into our bodies. Do we want fries with that? Sure we do! Fries taste good! But do we really need to eat them for every meal, not to mention super-size everything in sight? It's just not healthy. It's called portion control, folks, and we need to start toning it down some and getting back to regular levels. No one is a fan of counting calories, but it's time we started learning more about what we're eating, how much we're eating, and balancing both of those with a little bit of physical activity too. That means reading the labels on food from time to time. What is partially hydrogenated corn oil anyway? What is all this artificial flavoring stuff that's in our snacks and what is it doing to our bodies? Rather than grabbing those chips and sodas, why not try some healthy alternatives like adding more fruits and veggies to our diets? And no, the piece of lettuce, slice of tomato, and the pickle that comes with your burger doesn't count. It's time to remember that not everything has to be fried, dipped, or processed to taste good. Sometimes a fresh ear of corn can be just as yummy as those deep-fried corn chips. So take back your waistline! There are countless resources out there dedicated to developing healthier eating habits and starting the fat fight today. Below are a few to get you going.

 VISIT

www.eatingwell.com
www.webmd.com/diet
www.mypyramid.gov

 **WATCH**

The Morgan Spurlock documentary *Supersize Me* (2004)

27. Learn How to Cook

Hey, Top Chef. What you cooking? What? The closest you've come to preparing a meal is adding milk to your cereal? Then it's time for you to learn how. It's not only an awesome way to impress your friends, but it also ensures you know exactly what you're eating and how it's prepared. Who wants to eat high fructose propylene glycol butylated hydroxytoluene anyway? If you're just getting started, buy Mark Bittman's *How to Cook Everything*. It's a must-have food bible that will show you how to make it all, from roasted chicken to a perfectly executed poached egg. Mark's philosophy is that food can be delicious and healthy, and often the best recipes are those that are made from five items or less, which is perfect for all you newbies out there. And for all you veggie lovers, he speaks your language too: *How to Cook Everything Vegetarian*. Yum.

 **VISIT**

www.howtocookeverything.tv
www.amateurgourmet.com
www.smittenkitchen.com
www.epicurious.com

 WATCH

The Food Network

 READ

How to Cook Everything: Simple Recipes For Great Food by Mark Bittman

28. Get More Sleep

How would you like the ability to have über-concentration that would put Ritalin to shame? You say you'd like a stronger immune system too? What if we told you you could have all this and more and it was absolutely free? What is this miracle drug you say? It's called sleep. And most of us don't get enough, which is why we end up sleepwalking through our lives rather than living them to the max. Sleep is one of the most important things we can do for our bodies, our minds, and our souls. So turn off *The Late Show* and get to bed. Thanks to your DVR and YouTube, you can get a great night's rest and catch it tomorrow with the added bonus of being able to fast forward through Letterman's not-so-funny monologue if you want.

Having problems catching those zzz's? Are the worries keeping you up at night? Here are a few tips to get you counting sheep in no time:

- Exercise. Sorry folks, but once again it's time to hit the gym. It not only makes you feel better mentally and makes you look better in a bikini or Speedo, but it helps you sleep better too. Guess it's time to renew that membership at the Y.
- Say bye-bye to the booze, caffeine, and smokes. Unfortunately what's bad for you during the day also affects how you sleep at night. Alcohol can help you fall asleep faster, but it subsequently makes your quality of sleep less. Caffeine—surprise, surprise—does what it was designed to do: it keeps you awake. And cigarettes with their habit-inducing nicotine act as a stimulant, also a no-no if you want to get a good night's rest.
- Turn off the TV and pick up a book. *24* rocks, but it also can keep you up at night. Sorry, Kiefer.

Now put us down and get some shut-eye, will ya? See you tomorrow. You're getting very, very sleepy. . . .

CHAPTER 3

SOUL

29. Be an Optimist

66

"Hope is the bedrock of this nation; the belief that our destiny will not be written for us, but by us; by all those men and women who are not content to settle for the world as it is, who have the courage to remake the world as it should be."
—President Barack Obama (January 3, 2008)

99

Yes we can! Yes We Can! YES WE CAN! We certainly got to hear that line plenty of times leading up to November 4,

2008. But aside from being a catchy not-so-little campaign slogan, there's something in that phrase that obviously captivated the hearts and minds of the American people: hope and optimism. Optimism is an incredibly powerful tool, especially when we are faced with uncertain times. It allows us to look for opportunities rather than roadblocks in trying circumstances. President Obama's election and inauguration seemed to usher in a new era of optimism, one that people seemed to be craving for. How else can you describe the spontaneous celebrations that spilled into the streets on election night in cities and towns across the country? But in fact, the notions of hope and optimism are what this nation was founded on, tracing all the way back to our Founding Fathers. Adversity, change, and transition are never easy to deal with, but you might be surprised that what might seem like disaster at first can actually lead to amazing new avenues in life. So when given the choice to look at a situation either with the glass half empty or half full, why not choose the latter? There's no telling where the power of positive thinking can take you.

 READ

Always Looking Up: The Adventures of An Incurable Optimist by Michael J. Fox (He talks about how living with Parkinson's disease changed his perspective in life for the better.)

Long Walk to Freedom: The Autobiography of Nelson Mandela by Nelson Mandela

 WATCH

The film *The Shawshank Redemption* (1994) starring Tim Robbins and Morgan Freeman

The video "Randy Pausch's Last Lecture: Achieving Your Childhood Dreams" on YouTube

30. Find Your Personal Faith

"Faith is not just something you have, it's something you do."

—President Barack Obama (December 1, 2006)

Religion sure is in the hot seat these days. From the war in the Middle East to the war of words here in the States over Pastor Rick Warren speaking at the inauguration, it's pretty obvious that we're living in a world filled with people who believe in many different things. What we love best about President Obama is not only his efforts to practice inclusion no matter someone's race, politics, or sexual orientation, but also his views on religion, more specifically faith. It's important to believe in something, and the choice is yours; there's a whole menu of things out there to choose from. Don't let the word "religion" get in the way of what it means to have faith. Spirituality or the practice of yoga as a way to get in touch with your soul is just as important as Judaism, Christianity, and Islam.

Not well versed in God, whatever s/he may be? Take a religion class at your local community college and learn about all the many faiths that are out there. Spirituality not in your repertoire? Take a Kundalini yoga class and listen to what the gurus have to say. It's great to learn about how many options we have to choose from.

31. Go on a Vision Quest

A good thing to try if you find yourself unable to answer some of those bigger-than-life questions, like "What do I believe in?" is to stop and sit with your thoughts. And the best way to do that is to get out of your daily routine and take some time to figure it all out. We're not suggesting you find a Native American and head out into the desert like our friend Jim Morrison did in *The Doors* movie; simply find a weekend to be alone. It can be in your own apartment, or better yet, somewhere in the woods. Rent a cabin or pitch a tent and sit with the most awesome person in the world—you. Try to think about what's important to you and why. Try to listen to your inner voice and hear what it's saying now that you're alone. You can also try to set some goals for yourself that you want to try to achieve in the next month, six months, a year, and five years after you've spent a time-out from all the distractions of life. So next time you're faced with a big decision or find yourself having unanswerable questions in the middle of the night, consider taking a mini vision quest. You'll be amazed at how powerful some alone time can be to not only your psyche, but your soul too.

 READ

Walden by Henry David Thoreau (Get a sense of a big-time journey into living alone.)

32. Meditate

While we're talking about vision quests and taking more time to be alone, we should probably mention the easiest way to tap into the inner you: the art of meditation. Taking some time to sit in silence can lower stress, anxiety, and help you have more focus in all areas of your life.

MEDITATION 101

Though a variety of meditation techniques exist, there are basic elements that anyone can master. Doing as little as ten minutes per day is enough to feel results.

1. Sit or lie in a comfortable position with your eyes closed.
2. Focus your attention on the repetition of a word, sound, phrase, or prayer, doing this silently or whispering. An alternative is to focus on the sensation of each breath as it moves in and out of your body.
3. Every time you notice that your attention has wandered (which it will inevitably do), gently redirect it back, without judging yourself.

Need some help shutting down your thoughts? Music is a great way to guide your inner self into stillness. Check out **newearthrecords.com** where they have a plethora of mind-quieting sounds to get you relaxed in no time at all. How about a guru to guide you? He doesn't just make weird movies, he also believes in the power of meditation! Filmmaker David Lynch has set up a nonprofit organization dedicated to providing funds for students to learn to meditate through Transcendental Meditation teaching: Check out the David Lynch Foundation for more information on ways you can get involved.

 VISIT

www.newearthrecords.com
www.davidlynchfoundation.org
www.learningmeditation.com (for more tips on mastering the art of Om)

33. Dig for Your Roots

So, who are you? We mean, beyond your profiles on MySpace and Facebook and Twitter? Who are you *really*, and where do you come from? Take a cue from our president, who took his own journey of self-discovery to Africa when he was in his twenties to visit his father's homeland, and get in touch with your roots. With modern DNA testing, you can swab your cheek, pop it in the mail, and trace your DNA to thousands of years ago to see where you really came from. And with today's databases and catalogues, you can find your great-great-great Grandma and Grandpappy Pittipooh's names on the registrar at Ellis Island before they started on their covered wagon journey out west. Or if you're the adventurous type, talk to your family, gather as much information as you can, and jump on a plane to do some exploring on your own.

 VISIT

www.ancestry.com (to get started on tracing your family tree)
www.kindredkonnections.com
www.ellisisland.org (to see if you can find when and where your family's American journey began)
www.familytreedna.com (to see how you can get your DNA tested)
www.africanancestry.com

 RESEARCH

See if your motherland or fatherland offers subsidized trips for young people through the government. For example, if you happen to be of Chinese descent, look

> into the Taiwan Study Tour (a.k.a. "Love Boat"), or if
> you're Jewish, head over to Israel through the birth-
> right program (**www.birthrightisrael.com**).

34. Nurture Your Family-and-Friend Tree

Friends and family are forever. And sometimes we don't
realize how important they are until an unexpected event
happens and we really need them. But we think every day is
the day to recognize our loved ones for the rocks that they
are. So start getting to know those you love a little bit better.
Pick up the phone and call your cousin in Cleveland who
you haven't seen since last Thanksgiving. Or plan a mini
family reunion for next summer. Feel free to print up some
classic reunion T-shirts even if there are only four of you.

For all you only children out there, families don't have
to have the same genes. You can create your own family
tree with friends and coworkers *as well as* those sharing
your DNA. We love the idea behind urban tribes. Urban
tribes are groups of friends who observe regular rituals
together, and provide the support of an extended family
all while living in the same community. Wow! Sounds
great to us! So why not form your own urban tribe and
celebrate next Passover together if you find you can't

make it home that year? And hey, who says you have to be Jewish to celebrate Passover? Attending a Seder is a great way to not only spend some time with friends but also learn more about Jewish heritage, tradition, and culture at the same time. Not to mention you'll get the chance to eat one of the greatest foods in the world, matzo ball soup!

Here's another idea: Why not combine two great tastes that are even better together? Family and volunteering. Sign up for some volunteer work with your genetic family or the one created by you. Volunteer Family is an organization that matches you and your "family" with volunteer experiences sure to be the talk of next year's holiday feast. And they define "family" very loosely, so you and your four cube-mates totally count.

While you're at it, why not start developing some new relationships by inviting more people to the proverbial party called life? Make plans with someone new rather than always relying on your standby crew. Try to invite a few not-so-familiar faces every time you have a party. For all you Girl Scouts out there the "make new friends but keep the old, one is silver and the other gold" mantra still holds very true.

At the end of the day there is nothing more powerful than a group of people you can rely on and look to every time you're trying to do something challenging or new, or straight up fun. So start trolling those Facebook pages and ask one of those 584 "friends" to lunch.

 VISIT

www.urbantribes.net (the place for you and your handpicked family tree to meet others and learn about events in your hometown)
www.volunteerfamily.org

35. Live Simply

If you're like us, you're constantly busy and on the go. Work, school, friends, family, gym, dates, vacations, shopping, TV, Facebook, Twitter, the list goes on and on. It seems like we're swimming in obligations and goals, constantly treading water just to keep up. It's a fast-paced world we live in, especially these days, and sometimes it feels like it's overwhelming for even the best of us. So have you ever considered going back to basics and simplifying things a bit? You know, living life by the K.I.S.S. principle (Keep It Simple Stupid) that we all learned in eighth grade English class when we were writing essays. Did you ever think what you might discover if you turned your "CrackBerry" off for a bit? Or if you forego those designer jeans and pocket the cash instead? There can be something very calming about cutting out the clutter in our lives and living more simply. Sounds crazy, we know, but clutter and mess can actually add to our stress levels. We don't really need all the things that we *think* we need. So why not consider slowing down for a bit and just try to live simply? You'll save some money, have more time for yourself, and probably have more peace of mind too. And remember, more isn't always better; sometimes it's just more.

 VISIT

www.simpleliving.net
www.eartheasy.com (search "livesimply")
www.getmoredone.com (search "tips")

 READ

Voluntary Simplicity by Duane Elgin

36. Give a Little

The old saying that goes "'tis better to give than receive" wouldn't be an old saying if there weren't some truth to it. We all love getting gifts on our birthday or during the holidays, but it truly is a great feeling to be in a position to help someone when we can. Giving, in whatever form it takes, is a way of putting positive energy out there in the world, and hopefully one day that same energy will come back to you again.

Giving money to a charity not only helps you feel good, but also is invaluable to a nonprofit's ability to stay up and running. It doesn't have to be a lot, even a donation of a few dollars can make a difference. So go ahead and forfeit that latte once a week and give to some cause that you really believe in. Can't figure out who to give to? Check out Bringlight (**www.bringlight.com**) They'll not only help you find places that need your help, but they will also screen every charity on their site to validate their legitimacy. You can also track how the money you donate is helping and see what others who have joined the community are giving to.

And don't forget about that all-important commodity known as time. In some ways, giving your time can be much more valuable than any monetary donation you can make. There are plenty of opportunities for you to volunteer in your community. A great place to get started are the Web sites **serve.gov** and **volunteermatch.org**, which allow you to put in your location and a cause you are interested in volunteering with, and they will put you in touch with an organization that could use an extra pair of hands like yours.

Want to give more than money and time? How about your career? You could always get a job working for a nonprofit. Get paid to make the world a better place! Sounds pretty great to us. Check out Idealist, an organization that lists all sorts of nonprofit opportunities and organizations that are looking to hire socially motivated people just like you. Let's give it up for giving!

 **VISIT**

www.serve.gov
www.volunteermatch.org
www.bringlight.com
www.idealist.org

READ

Giving by president Bill Clinton

37. Appreciate Nature

Cars honking, phones ringing, and jackhammers hammering are part of the exciting soundscape of city life. It's great to be a city slicker, but nothing puts the day-to-day grind into perspective quite like getting back to nature. With the birds chirping, brooks babbling, and leaves rustling, nature can really make the daily hub-bub of life seem pretty insignificant. Sometimes it can seem like we're so rushed just trying to get through the day that we can't even hear ourselves think. But if you really want the grand perspective of things, take a stroll through the woods or take a hike through a wilderness park. The sights and sounds of nature can just melt all that other stuff away and make our problems at work or school seem very, very small. It's easy to get wrapped up in our fast-paced technology-driven lives, and we can forget that we're all just part of the giant web of life that goes on around us every day. So if you're feeling stressed out or just need a break, consider planning a camping trip or even just take a hike for a few hours to get away from it all. Now we know that camping in the backcountry is not for everyone, but it sure can be a great adventure if you have the time or inkling. So stop once in a while and escape back to nature to literally smell the flowers. We promise it'll do you good.

VISIT

www.nps.gov (to find a park or campground near you)

READ

A Walk in the Woods by Bill Bryson

WATCH

The film *Dances with Wolves* (1990) starring Kevin Costner

38. Practice the Art of Saying "Yes. And . . ."

Bored of the same old routine? Tired of never doing anything new? Well, it's time to break out of it! We know we sound like an infomercial when we say that, but most of us live in our own little bubbles and we all have our own routines which we can feel trapped in. But all we really have to do is tweak our habits just a little bit, and say "yes" when we normally would say "no," and we'll be surprised at the new possibilities that come our way. Try it and you'll see. People are creatures of habit, and it takes a lot sometimes for us to get motivated to do something different. But if you just open yourself up to new possibilities, and say "yes" to things that might force you out of your comfort zone, you might just jump start your way to exciting new adventures. Just ask Danny Wallace, who himself was in a funk until he took the advice of a stranger to say yes more often. So he decided to say "yes" to everything that came his way. And as fate would have it, he ended up with a book and movie deal out of it! Okay, so that's probably not going to happen for the rest of us, but it's still a great example of the possibilities that the universe has in store if you just open yourself up to them more. At the very least, you'll meet new people, have new experiences, go on new adventures, and learn new things. Sounds pretty good to us. And remember, we are Generation Change, after all, and what's our motto again? Yes we can!

READ

Yes Man by Danny Wallace

WATCH

The film *Yes Man* (2008) starring Jim Carrey

39. Flex Your Creative Muscles

Just because you can't draw doesn't mean you're not capable of being creative. Too often society puts these labels on us from an early age that say we're either creative types or noncreative types. We think if you can go out and pick up the mic and sing "All Night Long" by Lionel Richie at a karaoke bar, then that makes you a creative person. Besides, you shouldn't let a silly label prevent you from exploring all the wonderful mediums creativity has to offer. Be it playing music, writing poetry, or acting in your community theater's production of *Cats*, we think every person should practice the art of being creative on a daily basis.

The first step is to choose what you're most interested in. Always wanted to play guitar and sing the blues? Then start by taking a guitar lesson and learning a few basic chords. You'll be surprised that knowing three easy chords like E major, A minor, and D7 can pretty much put you in line to play a whole host of hits! Have dreams of writing a novel? Start by practicing writing in a journal or a personal blog every day just to get the words flowing. What we're trying to say here is, those first baby steps to get you moving toward the end goal of being an artiste are never as difficult as the mind makes them. The longer you've been telling yourself that you're not creative, the harder it is to break the mental cycle that's stopped you from trying before. But we think now is the time to tell the internal naysayers that you're a creative soul and they better step aside because you've got some artistic things to do!

VISIT

www.theartistsway.com

READ

The Artist's Way by Julia Cameron

40. Be Happy. With You.

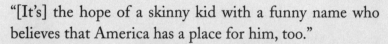

"[It's] the hope of a skinny kid with a funny name who believes that America has a place for him, too."
—President Barack Obama (July 27, 2004)

It's so easy to look in the mirror and see what's wrong. We're too short, too tall, too fat, or too thin. Even if you take the mirror out of the equation it's easy to let those insecurities run rampant at 3 A.M. when you can't sleep. That nagging inner critic loves to chatter in the middle of the night: "You're not smart enough, dedicated enough, and what do you have that's really going to make a difference?" The fact of the matter is there is no one more important, or able to make the world a better place than *you*. Think how boring the planet would be if we all were exactly the same? We've seen *The Stepford Wives* and that doesn't seem like a place we'd like to live. Look at President Obama. How do you think he bucked the political norm to become president of the United States of America? If he had stopped and listened to all the naysayers who said there was no way he could win—he was too black, too liberal, too young—we wouldn't have gotten the best thing to hit politics since sliced bread changed the whole sandwich game. Thankfully he ignored all the critics and chose to follow his own gut that told him he could be whatever he wanted to be and much more. And look how lucky we are as a result! Don't let *you* stop you from changing the planet as we know it. We can't wait to see what you come up with!

 READ

The Art of Happiness: A Handbook for Living by His Holiness the Dalai Lama and Howard C. Cutler

41. Set Some Goals for Yourself

So who out there made and kept a New Year's resolution last year? Um, nope, not us. And why is that? Well, partially because we're too busy partying the night away to remember any resolutions we made the night before. But also because New Year's isn't when we traditionally set the big goals for ourselves; those probably take a longer time to bring into focus than one night. We all obviously have goals in life, but sometimes it's not easy to figure out how to accomplish them. Trust us, we're right there with you. What we've found that helps is writing them all down. Consider these thoughts about goal setting:

- Be passionate about what you want to achieve, then set your goal.
- Make sure you write down what you want in detail and what steps you need to take to get closer to achieving it.
- Set your bar high. Don't aim low.
- Stay positive about your goals. List what you want, not what you *don't* want.

Thinking about goals in this way makes them more real, and it's a great feeling to cross them off when we actually reach them. It works in all parts of our lives, for the long run or the short run, and in our professional and personal lives. Sure, it can be hard to figure out the real long-term stuff, as it can all seem too fuzzy when it's not just around the bend. But do you really think President Obama thought he was going to be president when he was a freshman in college? It's important to aim high and keep them in sight, so that you can slowly start inching your way toward them. The short-term stuff is much easier. For example, say you would like to become a better runner, then your checklist might go like this: Get off the couch. Check. Put on running shoes. Check. Stretch. Check. Get outside and run. Check. Break a six-minute-mile pace. Hmmmm, might take a little longer to do. But if you write your goals down and make a mental note that you *will* get there (always think in the positive), maybe not today, or tomorrow, but someday, it will be like lighting a fire under your butt. When you have a goal set, it's easier to focus and figure out what steps you need to take to accomplish it. Now if only we all had personal soccer announcers on hand to yell "Gooooooooooooooooooooooaaaaaaaaaaal!" every time we crossed one off our list. That would really kick ass! Check out the following Web sites for some goal-setting tips.

 VISIT

www.mygoals.com
www.about-goal-setting.com
www.topachievement.com/goalsetting

42. Practice Persistence

"I'm a big believer in persistence."
—President Barack Obama (March 24, 2009)

Whether he's dealing with the economy or restructuring the nation's healthcare system, our president is a big believer in practicing persistence. And he's not alone. Remember that "genius is one percent inspiration and ninety-nine percent perspiration" quote hanging in your ninth grade science classroom? Well that was Thomas Edison and he was preaching the power of pluck, tenacity, and endurance. In other words, don't give up. Never give up. You've got an idea that is going to change the world and make it a better place? You think that's going to be an easy thing to sell? The answer is no. But that doesn't mean it's not going to be the best idea ever! If you believe in something, then make it happen. No matter how long or hard the journey seems, the end result will make all that tough work worthwhile.

 WATCH

The film *Rudy* (1993) starring Sean Astin

> The film *Rocky* (1976) starring Sylvester Stallone. "Yo Adrian!"

43. Be Polite

Have you ever noticed when you get extraordinary customer service in a restaurant? You feel great, but then you walk outside and get the finger from the guy who cuts you off in the crosswalk. Nice. Not everyone needs to be Miss Manners, but there's something to be said about some common courtesy. Lady, we don't need to hear all the details about how wasted you got last night while you gab on your cell phone. And dude, stop texting your buddies at the dinner table—and start paying attention to your date! Overall, this country is a pretty friendly and polite place, but that doesn't mean we can't still make some improvements. Rather than being a jerk, why not offer your seat on the bus to that elderly gentleman or that pregnant woman? And if someone bumps into you at a bar, don't try to start a fight to prove your manhood, dude, you'll just seem like a tool. And ladies, don't gossip about your friends—it's gonna come back to haunt you. So go ahead and hold the door open for that person behind you, offer to help that old lady cross the street, and greet the cashier in the checkout lane. And *hello*, turn off your cell phone in the theater—it's only two hours of your life, people! All these little things help make America a better place, and like the old saying goes, good manners cost nothing. So try to be polite, even when other people aren't. Please?

44. Champion a Cause

Having difficulty finding an organization that shares your passion for proving the existence of the Florida skunk ape? Well then why don't you champion a cause to alert people to the problem? Who says you can't start your own movement? Starting a nonprofit may sound daunting, but finding a cause that's being neglected and getting others on the bandwagon *can* be done. Check out **thepoint.com**, a Web site designed to walk you through what you need to do to influence change and connect to others. Next thing you know you'll be making public service announcements with Brad Pitt and you'll be the talk of the town. What you waiting for? Get thee to a computer and start alerting the masses!

 VISIT

www.thepoint.com

45. Pick Up the Phone

Remember that thing called a phone call? It's what your iPhone does when you're not using it to surf the Web, send texts, or update your Twitter feed. It seems like Mr. Telephone is rapidly becoming the handwritten letter of our generation. Unless you're video chatting every time you need to talk to someone, we spend most of our time talking *at* people, rather than with them. So, next time you find yourself thinking about an old friend from high school, don't be so quick to jump on Facebook and post on their wall, instead try picking up the handset and using your voice to show you care. You'll be surprised at how nice it feels to be able to have a conversation longer than 140 characters and typo free.

Hate the idea of paying money to talk? If you haven't heard, there's an awesome new sheriff in town and her name is Skype. With her, calls and video calls, as well as IM, are totally free.

 VISIT

www.skype.com

46–55. Ten Not-So-Deep-or-Earth-Shattering-Changes That Still Make a Difference

Sometimes change doesn't have to be a big deal. There are little things you can do on a daily basis that only require the commitment of practicing them to make them work. Try a few of these on for size. They're sure to make your body, mind, and soul feel really great.

46. Don't Worry So Much. Everything Will Work Out.

Try to have faith that every dark cloud will eventually pass. They always do, just not as quickly as we'd like them to sometimes. And behind every rainstorm there's always a ray of sun. So try to keep that in mind and put those 4 A.M. worries to bed. For good.

47. Kick Cursing to the Curb.

We all do it. But we all wish we did it less. So let's actually do it less.

48. Enjoy the Sunshine. With Sunscreen.

The sun not only gives us light, which can improve our moods, but it gives you the added value of vitamin D, too. Just don't forget the requisite SPF to protect you from those nasty UV rays.

49. Don't Be Too Critical of Yourself. Or Others.

Tell the inner critic to take a hike. Forever. There's no need to beat yourself or others up anymore.

50. Always Stay Young at Heart.

We'll all get old one day, but your soul knows no age. Treat it like a kid and it will play forever. Tell yourself you're too old, and you'll start to believe it.

51. Floss. Not Sexy, but Necessary.

Brushing is to teeth what flossing is to gums. In other words, essential.

52. Talk About It. Whatever "It" Is. With Your Family, Friends, or Therapist

No need to be stoic here, people. It's okay to talk about your feelings—the good, the bad, and everything in between. Make sure you've got a go-to person who won't judge you and is open to listening every now and again. Learn to let that person know how you feel, because there's no good reason to keep things bottled up.

53. Trust Your Gut.

You know *you* better than anyone else does. Try not to forget it.

54. Watch a Sunset.

Beauty is only a skyline away. And it's waiting for you to watch it. It's a great way to take in the end of the day and think about all the wonderful things you want to do tomorrow.

55. Be On Time.

Why rush? Why make your friends wait? Why not get a watch?

SECTION II
Change Our Country

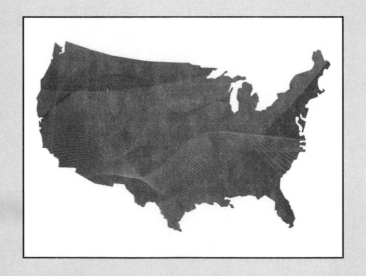

"**E**ach and every time, a new generation has risen up and done what's needed to be done. Today we are called once more—and it is time for our generation to answer that call. For that is our unyielding faith—that in the face of impossible odds, people who love their country can change it."
—President Barack Obama (February 10, 2007)

President Obama's election changed the face of this country forever. But there's a lot more left to do than just changing its face. Don't get us wrong, we love the face-lift that it has undergone, but we think it could use some more work, like a tummy tuck and some lipo, too, perhaps? All kidding aside, we think this country is pretty awesome already. So with a little work, imagine how much more awesomer it could be! Yeah, that's right, we said *awesomer*. Americans come in all shapes, colors, and sizes, and that's the beauty of this country. With all of us pitching in and working together, there's no limit as to what we can do. Fired up yet? Good! Now put your boots on and dig in to these next ideas to get that change a changin'!

CHAPTER 4

THE HOUSE OF YOU

56. Know What's Going on in Government

Okay. So just to throw a few numbers at you: Around $142 billion have been given to Bank of America, $280 billion to Citigroup, and $180 billion to AIG to help them stay afloat during this recession. And these numbers were close to accurate at press time, so who knows where they are now. That's your money, people! A bailout to help save the American economy has to come from somewhere, and usually that place is your paycheck. Unfortunately, that's the beauty and the downside of the way our great country is set up. In other words, we all work together to help one another out and sometimes that means pitching in with some good old-fashioned cash to make it happen. So we think it's of the utmost importance to know where your dollars are going. You certainly wouldn't hand your life savings over to your cousin Larry and not ask him where he was going to spend it, so why would you do it with Uncle Sam?

We say, watch out Washington, we see you! Become an active watchdog of America and find out what's really going on in the White House. Read the papers, but also do some research of your own; it's your right as an American citizen, so take what's yours. When he was a senator, the president helped pass a law, the Federal Funding Accountability and Transparency Act, which was meant to bring average Americans a kind of "Google" for the federal government. It basically makes it easier for us to look up any company or organization that's receiving federal contracts or money from Uncle Sam. It's your hard-earned tax money after all, so you better know where it's going!

VISIT

www.usaspending.gov
www.google.com/enterprise/government

57. Watch the Presidential News Conferences

This may sound simple. And stupid. But in this era of pre-packaged information coming at you twenty-four hours a day, it's sometimes good to remember your opinion doesn't just count, it's of the utmost importance. The next time our president has a news conference, watch it. Try to resist the urge to find out what blahblahblah.com or the *Huffington Post* has to say and try to form your own opinion first. Then when it's all over, it's all fair game. Unleash the beast that must read every political blog known to man. Or attempt to stay on CNN as they dissect every single word, gesture, and paragraph with the "best political team out there." Or better yet, invite your newly founded urban tribe over for a presidential news conference party and put some of those new debate and cooking skills to practice. Bringing people together is a wonderful way to hear different opinions about what's going on while it's happening.

And the good news is that your friend Daniel is a lot more likely to help you wash dishes afterwards, which is more than we can say for James Carville!

Missed some of those great speeches, news conferences, or press events in the past? Luckily our friends at the White House post all their greatest video hits in one spot for your viewing pleasure at **vimeo.com**.

VISIT

www.vimeo.com/whitehousevideos

58. Adopt a Pet

Pets are the best. They're there for you when you've had a bad day or when you're sick. They don't care if you've got bad breath or if your hair is a mess. In other words, they have unconditional love that can't be beat. Not to mention the health benefits from snuggling with a four-legged creature. Having a pet not only lowers your stress levels but it can help ward off cardiovascular disease too. But the sad truth is that five million dogs and cats are needlessly killed in U.S. shelters every year. And every puppy purchased from a pet store means that one more furry friend from a shelter will never find a home. How sad is that? Pet store pups are usually products of puppy mills, which are inhumane breeding machines. Don't forget that having a pet is a ten-to-fifteen-year commitment, so don't just run to the shelter every time you're feeling depressed or lonely. But if you find yourself with a little extra love and time to give back, then adopting might be for you. And don't forget to support the causes that are making sure all the homeless puppies and kitties are being cared for!

Need help finding a shelter to adopt your soon-to-be new best friend from? **Petfinder.com** has listings for shelters all across the great fifty states. And if you're interested in volunteering or even donating to help animals in the shelter system, check out the ASPCA and the Humane Society, both of which are the go-to resources that help make our four-legged friends' lives a little better.

Allergic? Live in an apartment that doesn't allow pets? You too can still enjoy the wonder that is pet ownership! Go to YouTube and type in "cat." Or "dog." Bet you got a listing for a video that's been made in Japan that has close to a million hits. And we know you're probably laughing hysterically as we write but dander allergy or pesky landlord be damned!

VISIT

www.aspca.org
www.hsus.org
www.petfinder.com

---

59. Plant a Garden

With all this talk about President Obama, we want to make sure we give a shout-out to our great First Lady, Michelle Obama! She's the ultimate example of style and grace and perfectly complements the president at the head of our First Family. But she really caught our attention when we heard that she was planting a garden at the White House. Not since Eleanor Roosevelt back in WWII has there been a vegetable garden at 1600 Pennsylvania Avenue, and we think she's doing an incredible job setting an example for the country to follow. Planting a garden is a great exercise in discipline and patience, but it's also an incredible way to enjoy the literal fruits of your labor. There's nothing quite like eating fresh vegetables and fruits from a garden that you've worked on—somehow the food just tastes better. Not only is it healthy for you, as you're eating food straight from the vine with no chemicals or pesticides, but you're helping the environment and beautifying your neighborhood too. If you're really lucky, you might have your own yard to work in, but even if you live in a city, you can look into community garden plots where you can join your neighbors to till the earth. Or why not plant veggies in pots on your fire escape, window, or roof? Hey, if the president can find time to pull weeds, then so can you. Grab those gloves, get some seeds, and get your green thumb on! Check out these Web sites for tips on how to get started.

 **VISIT**

www.gardening.about.com
www.garden.org
www.gardenguides.com

60. Vote

When was the last time you voted in a local election or actually knew what a district candidate believed in? No judgments here folks, we're way guilty of it too. Too often we choose candidates based on what party they belong to, rather than what they're promising to bring to the office if they're elected. And the fact of the matter is some of the most important legislature that's getting passed stems from a local level. So take some time and find out who is representing you and add them as your friend on Facebook; that way you'll have a constant update as to what they're doing—they're working for you after all. And if they don't have a Facebook page, make sure to send them a typed letter welcoming them to the twenty-first century and showing them the ways of our new world.

Here's a crazy idea: Find out who represents you in Congress at **congress.org**, then invite them over for dinner and get to know them better! Better do it quick before they start the quest toward a higher candidacy. Okay, maybe that's a little too ambitious—besides we're not sure if those cooking skills of yours are up to snuff yet. Then at least take a look at their Web sites and see what platform they're running on and why they think they're the best person for the job. Or if you have some free time on your hands, why not volunteer in their campaign office for a few hours a week? What better way to learn what they're all about than by hanging out in their presence every once in a while?

This next Web site is dense, but it's only because it has so much invaluable info about what's going on in the government. So take an afternoon off from the soaps and dig into a little **usa.gov.** Your inner political junkie will thank you.

 VISIT

www.usa.gov

www.congress.org

www.declareyourself.com (where you can talk to others who share your political passion, get info about the topics that matter, and much, much more)

61. Appreciate Being an American

"What has always united us—what has always driven our people, what drew my father to America's shores—is a set of ideals that speak to aspirations shared by all people: that we can live free from fear and free from want; that we can speak our minds and assemble with whomever we choose and worship as we please."
—President Barack Obama (July 24, 2008)

If you've traveled to any of the other countries of the world, you know that there are some amazing places beyond our borders. The sights, the sounds, the cultures, and the people that you encounter when you leave the United States can be an incredible experience, but there's nothing quite like coming back home to the States. Sure we might have our problems, but America is still the beacon of hope and inspiration to the rest of the world, the epitome of all that is possible in life if people are given opportunity. And we think that's pretty sweet. The election of Barack Obama as our forty-fourth president highlights the fulfillment of an American dream as laid out in our Declaration of Independence, that "all men are created equal, that they are endowed by their Creator with certain unalienable Rights, that among these are Life, Liberty and the pursuit of Happiness." While this country is great in so many ways, from its land to its industries to its culture and to its people, what the world really admires most about us are the principles and ideals that this country was founded on, and that these principles and ideals are still embraced and held sacred to this very day. It's what drives people to want to move here, it's what attracts foreign students and professionals to our land, and it's the very foundation of what makes us such a strong country. We can agree to disagree with each other about how things are run, but make no mistake that at the end of the day, we should all consider ourselves very lucky to be able to call ourselves American. So wave that flag and be proud of our stars and stripes, because it represents all the possibilities that this great country holds for all of us.

62. Support Our Seniors

Senior citizens truly are a national treasure. They are the link from our present to our past, they are our parents and grandparents, and they can tell you what life was really like back in the day. Don't ever forget that they were young once too. Plus they have a lot more experience and wisdom than we could hope for, so if we listened to them for a moment we could all probably really learn something. It's not always easy getting older, and no amount of Botox is ever going to change that. Many times the elderly can end up alone or away from family, so why not spend some time volunteering to let them know that they aren't forgotten? Every town in America has a senior citizens center or nursing home, and most could always use an extra pair of hands, a teacher for a class, or a smiling face to greet the residents. Don't have time to commit at that level? Consider supporting the AARP, the country's leading nonprofit organization dedicated to working on issues that are important for Americans fifty and older. But if you really want to make a senior's day, the best thing that you can do is pick up the phone and call your parents or grandparents or an aunt or uncle right now. You don't need a reason. Just call to say "hi."

VISIT

www.aarp.org

63. Have an Emergency Plan

Overall we like to think that life is pretty sweet. But once in a while an event takes place that shakes the foundation of our very stability. We're talking about cataclysmic events like 9/11 and Hurricane Katrina that shock us so profoundly that the entire country is thrown for a loop. While we all do our best to keep our country safe, it's an unfortunate fact that we can't always predict the next disaster. But that doesn't mean there aren't precautions to take should the unthinkable happen near you. Keep in mind that it doesn't take much time or effort to get prepared, but the potential payoff could be lifesaving. The key to everything is three simple steps: have an emergency supply kit on hand, make a plan with your friends and family, and stay informed with what's going on near you. Doesn't sound too bad, right? Here are a couple of ideas to keep in mind:

- Don't worry about packing your Nintendo Wii in this emergency kit. Stick with the basic things you will need to survive: water, food, clean air, and warmth. After you've got those covered, think what else you might need like batteries, medicine, maps, flashlights, etc.
- Talk to your family about making a plan for different situations. You might not all be together if disaster strikes, so know where you can meet up, how you can reach each other, or where you will go.
- Stay up-to-date with what's going on near where you live. Is your area more prone to earthquakes or tornadoes? Do you live in a flood plain or near a power plant? The more you can plan for the likely possibilities in your area, the better off you'll be.

VISIT

www.ready.gov (for a complete list of ideas and information in regards to emergency situations)

64. Spend (and Save) Your Money Wisely

Wow, this recession really sucks. Where did all of our money go?! Where did all of our jobs go?! It's a brutal reality check that we're going through, and it's forcing all of us to readjust our spending habits. We're a country that loves to consume, but sometimes we end up buying and spending ourselves way into debt, and unfortunately digging out of that hole isn't always the easiest thing to do. And it's no fun either. Don't worry, we'll weather this storm as we always do, but let's learn something from our time on this financial roller coaster. We all could probably be a bit more responsible with our spending habits, but a lot of times we don't realize where all our money is going. Consider mapping out a monthly budget to track how much money you're spending on different things. Sometimes the revelations can be quite interesting. In other words, when your bar tab rivals your rent check each month, it might be time to evaluate your spending habits. That's not to say we shouldn't live the good life, but it's a pretty smart idea to tuck away some savings for a rainy day. Most experts agree that we should sock away anywhere from six to nine months' worth of savings in case we're hit with an unexpected incident that turns our world upside down. Check out more tips on how to wisely save and spend your benjamins at the Web sites below.

 VISIT

www.youngmoney.com
www.mint.com (free personal finance software)
www.betterbudgeting.com/frugalliving.htm
www.jeanchatzky.com (financial guru Jean Chatzky's blog)

CHAPTER 5

NEIGHBORHOOD

65. Shop Locally

What we put into our bodies is really important. And we all know that when it's possible, eating organic is the way to go. But did you know that about 39 percent of climate change is due to using oil, natural gas, and other fuels? Some of this energy is used for the processing, packaging, refrigeration, and transportation of food. And unfortunately, unless you're living somewhere below the equator, that means that organic banana you're eating in December had to fly on a really long flight from Ecuador, then take a twenty-four-hour truck ride to get to that organic grocery store you love to buy all your food from. Not to mention the boxes used to haul the banana from point A to B. That's one mega-sized carbon footprint just so you can eat that yummy pesticide-free Chiquita. Long story short is this: Buying locally grown food greatly reduces the energy and resources necessary to transport and store foods. And most small local farmers don't use the nasty pesticides and fertilizers that big-time growers do. That means eating locally is not only healthier, but it's better for the planet too. A win-win in our book!

Most localvores believe in the idea of eating seasonally, which means when you're pulling out those sweaters for winter you're eating root vegetables and fruits that can be stored for longer periods of time, like apples. And summertime means it's time to start eating beans and spinach and all those other yummy green veggies that love the warm sun. For finding those local farmers to buy from, try **localharvest.org**. It's a great Web site that will help you find farmers' markets, family farms, and other sources of sustainably grown food in your area all year long.

Lazy? Too busy to shop? Join a CSA, a.k.a. Community Supported Agriculture, which makes it easy for you to buy local and seasonal food directly from a farmer. How does it work? Farmers offer a certain number of "shares," or boxes of fruits or vegetables, to the public. A group of people in a community join up to buy a group of shares from one farmer who typically will deliver the goods once a week, which are then picked up by you, right in your own neighborhood. Yummy and easy! Find a CSA farm near you at **localharvest.org/csa** or **sare.org/csa**.

So next time you find yourself with a hankering for broccoli grown with love, head on over to your local farmer's market, invite a few friends over and make an afternoon of it. The world and your body will thank you.

 VISIT

www.localharvest.org
www.localharvest.org/csa
www.sare.org/csa

 READ

The Omnivore's Dilemma by Michael Pollan

66. Serve America Through AmeriCorps

"The idea is simple—America invests in you, and you invest in America. That's how we're going to ensure that America succeeds in this century."
—President Barack Obama (June 16, 2008)

So we've all heard of the Peace Corps, the famous program started in the '60s to get Americans to help out overseas. But in these times, it's also all about AmeriCorps. In sports terms, think of the Peace Corps as playing away, and AmeriCorps as playing on home court. Launched in 1993 by president Bill Clinton, AmeriCorps is about service and giving back to your country in local communities through a network of local and national nonprofit organizations. Each year, 75,000 AmeriCorps members work in the areas that need the most help across the nation such as education, public safety, health, and the environment. There are a lot of different ways to get involved—from part-time service in your town, to full-time residential placement away from home. And it's not just a volunteer program; many members receive a modest living allowance, and upon completion of the program you can qualify for an education reward that can go toward repaying student loans or other education expenses. And AmeriCorps is only going to get bigger from here. In 2009, President Obama signed into law the Serve America Act, which will expand Ameri-Corps from 75,000 positions to 250,000 positions over the next eight years. So how about it? Feel up to the task of serving your country? Then take a look at the Web site below to learn more.

VISIT

www.americorps.gov

67. Clean Up Your Community

If you're like us, you hate cleaning. Who doesn't really? But still, we gotta admit that the sight of our homes sparkling clean makes us feel pretty darn great. While it's relatively easy to make sure that our own homes stay clean, what about the larger community that we live in? Just like our homes, we have to live in it everyday and see it everyday, so we should take some pride in its upkeep too! There's an interesting school of thought, known as the Broken Windows theory, which says that if a window of a vacant house gets broken, and nobody fixes it right away, then the odds of another window getting broken by vandals get higher. Since nobody seems to care if the windows keep getting broken, more and more windows will break, which ultimately leads to the decline of the neighborhood, because it shows a rise in crime or a lack of caring or pride in the community. Do your part to keep your neighborhood clean and safe, because little things like keeping the trash out of the way and getting rid of graffiti can add up to make a mountain of difference. The Keep America Beautiful campaign has been around for years and has hundreds of local affiliates across the country that are dedicated to cleaning up and improving local communities. Focusing on issues like litter prevention, waste reduction, and beautification, this organization is a great place to learn more about how you can keep your neighborhood sparkling clean. Visit the Web site below and get in touch with your local affiliate today to see how you can get involved.

 VISIT

www.kab.org

READ

The Tipping Point by Malcolm Gladwell for more on the Broken Windows theory. Because who likes a drafty house anyway?

68. Write to Your Congressional Reps

You know the great thing about American government? Our leaders are all elected by you and me, which means they are accountable to *us*. That's right, we the people put them there. And every few years they need our votes to get elected or reelected. Don't forget that, since that's a pretty big deal. Whenever we feel powerless, and we all do from time to time, we have to remember that our voices *can* be heard, and changes *can* be made. But change always starts at the local level, so it's important to know who your local representatives are. Let them know what you're thinking. Because they represent your district or state, they should be more in tune and familiar with the issues and problems that you are dealing with in your community. Make your concerns known and write to your congressional representatives about them, and help keep our leaders accountable. Remember, it's *we the people*. And if you aren't happy with the way your district or state is being represented, well, there's always another election cycle just around the bend. Ain't democracy grand?

VISIT

www.house.gov/writerep
www.senate.gov

69. Be a Mentor

If you're lucky, you had a big brother or big sister in your life growing up. While they most likely made your life hell at some point, they also probably absorbed most of the slack from Mom and Dad before you had to. Not a bad deal, right? But they also inevitably influenced you in other ways that you don't even realize—whether it was sports, or studies, or career paths, or even just living up to their expectations, they can play a big part in our development. But a lot of kids don't have that positive older role model in their lives to look up to. And without that, many can go off course because they can't see their potential and what they can aspire to be. So even if you already have a little brother or sister in your family, you should consider becoming a mentor by donating some of your time to someone who doesn't. Even if you don't think you have much guidance or advice to give, you'd be amazed at how much a simple game of catch once in a while can affect a kid's life. There are smaller organizations and agencies on the local level in most communities that can pair you up with a kid in need, or larger national organizations like Big Brothers Big Sisters and the Boys and Girls Clubs of America. The Obama administration is making a concerted effort to make sure that kids know and understand the importance of an education and that they stay in school and graduate. A big part of being a mentor is just being there to help encourage and support kids as they go though the struggles of adolescence, which many times includes staying in school. So consider this as doing your part to fulfill an administration goal!

 VISIT

www.bbbs.org
www.bgca.org

 WATCH

The film *Role Models* (2008) with Seann William Scott
and Paul Rudd for a humorous take on this subject

70. Meet Your Neighbors

Nothing builds a sense of community like knowing who
lives next door or down the street. Not to mention it's
great to have a go-to person across the way when you absolutely need that cup of sugar at 3:00 A.M. And without his
neighborhood pals Glenn Quagmire and Cleveland Brown,
Peter Griffin's idiotic adventures on each episode of *Family
Guy* just wouldn't be as much fun. But these days it seems
that we live in increasingly isolated worlds away from our

neighbors. We may be chatting online with someone half a world away, but we might not know who lives across the hall or street from us. Well, that just doesn't seem right. So if you don't know them already, why not take the initiative and introduce yourself? Sure, it might seem a little strange and be a tad intimidating to just go knocking on doors out of the blue, so why not plan an event to get the whole neighborhood or building together? Potlucks and BBQs are a great tradition to start for a national holiday that gets everyone outside by the grill and chatting. Or go big and throw a block party with music and dancing, where you can really get your groove on with your neighbors! The fabric of this country starts at the local level, so get out there and start knitting up your neighborhood together.

 VISIT

www.meettheneighbors.org

WATCH

The documentary film *Dave Chappelle's Block Party* (2005) to see how the famous people get their fiestas going.

71. Tell a Story and Listen to Someone Else's

Nothing is more a part of our common humanity than the ancient art of storytelling. Pulling up to the proverbial campfire and telling a tale about something meaningful that's happened in your life is a great way to make sure our oral history continues to grow for many years to come. Think about it: your tale of canvassing for two weeks straight in October 2008 could be this generation's version of chopping down the cherry tree. Were you lucky enough to be in D.C. for the inauguration? Then take a few minutes and write it down. Just moved to a new city and find yourself meeting an unbelievable cast of characters every day? Did your dream from last night remind you of that time when you did something totally crazy? All this and more is story worthy, and the world is waiting to hear you tell it. And wouldn't it be nice to have something to tell your grandkids when they're old enough to ask what the world was like when you were their age? Details are of the utmost importance when you're telling tales so don't forget to add the embellishments that will take your story from zero to hero.

Feeling like you can't remember the art of creative writing from grade school? Take a class! Most community colleges offer short-story workshops where you can learn how to take real-life events and turn them into something sure to keep everyone on the edge of their seats. So stop making excuses and start weaving some tales, you Mark Twain, you!

 VISIT

www.writingclasses.com (They offer writing classes in both New York and Los Angeles as well as online.) **www.thisamericanlife.org** (Listen to this weekly radio show hosted by Ira Glass to hear one of the master storytellers at work.) **www.storycorps.net** (StoryCorps is a nonprofit project whose mission is to honor and celebrate one another's lives through listening and storytelling by recording your stories and airing them on public radio and the Internet.)

www.themoth.org (The Moth, another not-for-profit storytelling organization, has weekly podcasts as well as live events in major cities across the United States where you can listen to others' tales on selected topics.)

www.storycenter.org (Offers workshops to teach you how to make a digital story with pictures and video.)

72. Run for Office

Got a community issue that you think really deserves your full attention? One way to take your activism to the next level is to run for office. Sure it's like a one-in-a-number-too-big-to-even-imagine chance that you'll get elected as president of the United States, but if you aim your sights a little lower—and by lower we mean the local level—there's no reason why you can't run for office and win!

Here are a few steps to get you started:

- Research. Start by attending city or town council meetings and talking to people on the street as well as small business owners in your community. Find out what issues they feel are the most neglected by the current administration and start to really form your platform, i.e., what you stand for. Make sure you have a solid position on each issue you feel is important to your soon-to-be-formed campaign.

- Choose your opponent wisely. Like any race, you're not likely to win if there's a beloved incumbent or strong candidate on the ticket already. Find someone who hasn't been particularly popular with the people or who hasn't been faring well in the polls. You wouldn't expect to win a tennis match against Serena Williams, but how about her cousin John who has never picked up a tennis racket before? Sports tactics usually work well when you're talking politics.

- Collect endorsements. In other words, get local support before you actually put your name on the ticket.

- Sharpen those public speaking skills. Yup, there's that mastery of words again. How else are you going to convince people to vote for you if you don't have the gift of gab and the ability to confidently speak in front of a group?

- Clean up your closet. That means you need to be on your best behavior. Once you make the move into the public arena, all eyes are going to be on you and scrutinizing your every move. So it's time to button up that shirt and start living the goody-two-shoes life!

VISIT

www.runforoffice.org

READ

Campaign Boot Camp: Basic Training for Future Leaders by Christine Pelosi

73. Go on a Walkabout in Your Community

Google Maps and GPS systems are a beautiful thing. Essentially we never have to worry about getting lost again. That's amazing! But in another way it's also a little sad because sometimes you can find the coolest and most unexpected things when you get lost. So if you have time, why not stop worrying so much about getting directly from Point A to Point B and take the roundabout way? Or better yet, just wander even if you don't have a Point B to get to and take a walkabout. It's a great thing to do when traveling, but it can be even more profound if you do it near your home. If you're like us, and most of you probably are, you zip from place to place without giving much thought to what you pass along the way. It can be mind-blowing what you can see and learn and discover while taking your time to look around, especially if you do it on foot. So go ahead and try it—put on a comfy pair of walking shoes and just head out your door. Don't have a particular destination in mind, other than returning home eventually, and just start going. Wander. Let your feet guide you and see where you end up. You'll be amazed at what you see when you have time to stop and look around. Life will no longer be just a blur outside your car window, and more importantly, it will hopefully give you a better appreciation of the neighborhood or town in which you live.

 WATCH

The film *Lost in America* (1985) starring Albert Brooks

74. Support Mom-and-Pop Shops

Main Street America certainly looks different these days. Why is it that regardless of whatever city we go to, we always end up seeing the same brand-name shops, restaurants, and super stores? Whatever happened to some local flavor? Well kids, such is the changing landscape of American business, where many of us make our livelihoods working at huge companies. But in the fight of David versus Goliath, we can still support the underdog—the local store owned by mom-and-pop from around the way. Yeah, it might not be cheaper than its giant competitors, but mom-and-pop local shops are still the bread and butter of America. They help give a neighborhood its charm, a downtown its flavor, or a city its heritage, not to mention they keep the local economy going. Don't get us wrong, we shop at chain stores when we have to, but given the choice, why not root for the little guy? Without them, we'll all be eating the same thing, wearing the same clothes, and drinking the same drinks wherever we go. And that just seems a bit bland for our taste, dontcha think?

75–84. Practice 10 Random Acts of Kindness

Who says random can't make a difference? Try one of these ten ideas on for size and you're sure to make someone's day a bit brighter!

75. Walk Shelter Dogs/Pet Shelter Cats

If you can't adopt a pet, why not stop by your local shelter and give some love to a dog or cat waiting to find a home? It's so easy to spend a little time with a shelter animal while they're waiting to find their Daddy Warbucks. A lot of shelters have programs where you can help out by walking dogs so they can get exercise and fresh air, or play with a cute kitty so it can keep its pouncing skills sharp. So stop by your local shelter and tell them you've got some love to spare and you'd like to volunteer. Trust us, it will make a four-legged furry friend's day.

76. Make a Music Mix

Music rules. It's inspiring and awesome and will even make you dance on occasion. Next time you're looking for a way to do something nice for someone you love, like, or want to get to know better, why not give the gift of

music? Make a mix tape/CD or create a personal playlist
for someone online.

Need some inspiration? Check out the following links,
which are sure to get you up and making mixes in no time
at all!

 VISIT

www.imeem.com/tag/obama/playlists (Make a
playlist and dedicate it to the one we love.)
www.makeamixa.com (This little beauty looks like a
cassette but it's really a USB drive. Old school meets
new school. Now talk amongst yourselves.)
www.djztrip.com/obama (DJ Ztrip's mix is free
thanks to the Creative Commons. It mashes up
great music with some of Obama's most inspirational
speeches. Two great tastes that taste great together.)

77. Turn Off the Urge to Pay and Talk

Next time you're paying for something, try to avoid the
urge to multitask. In other words, just say no to simulta-
neous phone talking and coffee ordering. It's kind of rude,

not to mention it will surely hold up the line while you fumble to keep your mobile convo going while rifling for change. Baristas of the world will be singing your praises for years to come.

78. Tell Your Best Friend Thank You

"Thank You for Being a Friend" shouldn't just be the catchy theme song to the *Golden Girls* (rest in peace, Bea Arthur). It should be our daily mantra! When was the last time you told a good friend how much she means to you? More often than not, we seem to forget that friends deserve a little bit of gratitude. After all, they put up with us when we're happy, sad, and everything in between. Take five minutes and let someone close to you know how much you care. And don't be surprised if they say thank you back.

79. Bake Some Cookies

Who doesn't love some home-baked cookies every now and then? Surprise your office mates or your next-door neighbor with the gift of yum. Gym be damned—cookies rock! And we all know Keebler's got nothing on hand-baked with love. So turn up the heat on that oven and get stirring. All of your unsuspecting friends are going to be psyched.

VISIT

www.popularcookierecipes.com

80. Give Someone a Compliment

What if we said to you, "You look nice today. You're smart. I love your haircut. You're so funny! You write the most amazing and inspirational e-mails. Have you ever thought about being a writer?" Feels pretty good, doesn't it? Next time you're feeling like you've got some kindness to spare, why not dish it out to someone you know? Maybe she's doing something that you think is underappreciated or just looking particularly nice that day. Let's face it, we're all self-conscious at heart, and it feels really good to be appreciated for something we're doing or even how we're looking, especially if it comes out of the blue.

81. Pay the Toll for the Car Behind You

Next time you find yourself at a tollbooth, why not give a little extra and pay for the person behind you? How jazzed would you be if someone did the same for you? Now that's what we call random . . . because unless they've got crazy PI skills and can track you down via your license plate number, they'll never know who their benefactor was. Try it and the car behind you (let's hope it's a hybrid) will thank you! And if you find yourself in a land free of cars, try paying for the coffee for the person behind you next time you're in line at your local coffee shop. Cause when you're needing some caffeine, we think a gratis cup of java might feel just as good as a free stretch of interstate travel.

82. Give Up Your Seat for Someone on the Train or Bus

Sure, we all know it's just good manners to offer our seat to a pregnant woman or older person when we're riding public transportation, but how about offering up your seat to a stranger next time you're riding a crowded train at rush hour? It will be so unexpected they'll probably be talking about it for years to come. Try it, Joe Commuter might like it!

83. Give a Tip to Someone Working at a Drive-Thru

Just because it's called fast food, it doesn't mean it didn't take any time or effort to prepare. So why not give a tip to the person working at the drive-thru the next time you find yourself needing that milkshake at 3 A.M.? Tips are meant to say thanks for the service, and we think drive-thru employees deserve a little recognition too.

84. Shovel Someone's Snow

We just love a big ole snowstorm. There's something magical about that blanket of white falling upon our streets and lawns, let alone the prospect of school cancellations or an excuse to get to work late. But after the excitement of the impending snowball fight or skitch fest dies down, we're left with the reality of some unavoidable hard labor: having to shovel all that snow. And who likes that? Talk about a downer! So next time a blizzard decides to come to the party of life and you find yourself with a little extra shoveling energy, take a stab at a neighbor's sidewalk. They won't know how to thank you. If you're lucky it may involve some homemade, steaming hot chocolate. And for all of you living in the Sun Belt, feel free to randomly rake some leaves or mow someone's lawn. It's just as good.

CHAPTER 6

NATION

85. Send President Obama a Thank-You Note

This man has one hard job. He's not only a father and a husband but he's also the leader of the Free World. Talk about pressure. Why not send him a thank-you note and tell him how much you appreciate him? Keep the post office open and send a card. On recycled paper of course.

MAIL

President Obama
The White House
1600 Pennsylvania Avenue NW
Washington, D.C. 20500
www.whitehouse.gov/contact

VISIT

www.ithankobama.com (Send him a note now in anticipation for his second term! This site is gathering e-notes now and plans to publish them in 2013. Now that's what we call planning ahead.)

86. Be an American Ambassador When You Travel Abroad

Over the past few years, our country's rep hasn't exactly been its best ever. It's not that everybody hates us, but let's just say there's been one too many of us wearing

Canadian flags on our backpacks when we travel outside our borders. So how do we revamp our image? Just like any good politician knows, we need to be on our best behavior with the voters! And you can do that very easily when you travel abroad. All it takes is a few positive encounters with American tourists for the rest of the world to remember that we are still the generous, kind-hearted, and respectful nation that we've always been. Here are a couple of ideas you might want to chew on before you jump on that plane to parts unknown:

- Learn the language. This isn't an easy thing, but a few words or phrases go a long way.
- Learn the local customs and do as the locals do. Remember, drunken skinny-dipping in public fountains is usually frowned upon. In other words, don't be an American Borat.
- Respect the people and country where you are.
- Be friendly and humble.

Follow these basic tips and you're golden. We're all America's best publicists when we travel, so get out there and do your part. Being an ambassador has never been easier—and don't forget to swap out that maple leaf for the stars and stripes on your backpack!

VISIT

www.worldcitizensguide.org

---

87. Help the Homeless

Anywhere you go in America, be it big city or small town, you'll find people down and out on their luck with no place to go. Some of these folks have mental issues, some are substance abusers, but a lot of them are just regular people who've run into a string of unfortunate events that left them out on the streets. It's probably hard for most of us to imagine being homeless, but it's not as far fetched a notion as you might think. And consider this: some of the biggest names in Hollywood have spent some time during their lives down and out, including Halle Berry, Jewel, and Hilary Swank, to name a few. Even Captain Kirk (William Shatner) and James Bond (Daniel Craig) had it rough at one point in their lives. If it can happen to OO7 and the captain of the Starship Enterprise, it can happen to any of us. Have some compassion for those less fortunate the next time you see someone out on the streets or in need of shelter. Sure, giving some spare change or leftover food to a person in need is a quick fix, but also consider supporting national homeless advocacy organizations and local homeless shelters, soup kitchens, or clothing closets by volunteering your time or donating items or funds.

 **VISIT**

www.habitat.org
www.helpusa.org
www.nationalhomeless.org

88. Help Save the Arts in Schools

If you're like us, some of our best memories from school aren't ones of cramming for a math test or listening to a teacher ramble on and on about photosynthesis at 8 A.M. They're from our classes like music and art that gave us a break during the day from listening to a teacher lecture or reading from a book. But the sad fact is that arts programs are usually the first ones to get cut when budgets tighten up. And that means the sound of the school band echoing through the hallways gets silenced, the paintbrushes don't get dipped, and the pottery wheels stop spinning.

A school without the arts seems like a pretty sad place to be if you ask us. Studies show time and time again that art and music education help students develop key social and critical thinking skills. They also contribute to overall higher academic achievement for those who participate in them, and these kids are also less likely to drop out of school. So where the logic is in cutting these classes first, we have no idea. But as always, there are solutions to every problem. If you want to become an advocate for the arts, consider taking these steps:

- If you have kids or younger brothers and sisters who are still in school, ask what's going on with their arts programs and what you can do to get involved.
- Write or call Congress to tell them that you support more funding for the Arts in Education program.
- Support an arts advocacy organization by fund-raising for them or purchasing tickets to their events.
- Stay up-to-date with what's going on in education policy through these organizations to see what else you can do.

With your help, today's kids and tomorrow's kids will always get the chance to paint, draw, play, dance, and sing to their hearts content. Band geeks rule!

VISIT

www.artsusa.org

www.keepartsinschools.org

www.vh1savethemusic.com

WATCH

The film *Mr. Holland's Opus* (1995) starring Richard Dreyfuss

89. Honor Our Veterans

"Finally, there is one other thing that is not too late to get right about this war, and that is the homecoming of the men and women—our veterans—who have sacrificed the most. Let us honor their valor by providing the care they need and rebuilding the military they love. Let us be the generation that begins this work."

—President Barack Obama (February 10, 2007)

To quote an old Edwin Starr Motown song, "WAR! Huh. Good God ya'll. What is it good for? Absolutely nothing!" Yeah, we pretty much agree. War sucks. But sometimes the country ends up going to war, and we may or may not agree with that decision. Regardless of how we might feel about America's foreign policies, it's always important to support and respect our brave men and women in uniform and their families who are fighting for our country. Our soldiers don't make the policies that we may find divisive—they may not even agree with these policies themselves—but they are always there, doing their duty to keep us safe. They put their lives on the line and we owe them our utmost respect and gratitude when they come home. We have veterans now who are in their teens and early twenties, and we should do everything we can to welcome them home and give them all the support and help that they need to transition back into civilian life. So let's go beyond sticking that yellow ribbon bumper sticker on our cars, and consider welcoming troops home at the local airport, or sign up to drive a disabled veteran to where they need to go. And if you see men or women in uniform, make sure to thank them for their service to our country. Check out the following links to see what else you can do to help in your community.

VISIT

www.va.gov
www.dav.org
www.veteransandfamilies.org
www.iava.org

90. Support Our troops

Being away from home for a long time is always tough. You start to miss the little things: the familiarity of your surroundings, the comfort of family and friends, the smell and taste of home cooking. This can happen even when you're just traveling on vacation. So imagine what it's like for our men and women in uniform who are serving overseas for months and years at a time. They make sacrifices so that the rest of us can sleep more easily at night, so why not do something that lets them know that we're thinking about them and gives them a little taste of home? There are plenty of ways that you can do this. Send a care package, write a letter or a card, become a pen pal with a soldier, "adopt" a service person, anything that you can do to make a soldier feel a little more closer to home will help. It's the little things that can make a difference.

You don't need to know anyone personally serving in the military, either, because there are plenty of organizations and Web sites out there that can either match you with a soldier or make sure that your gift gets into the right hands. They will thank you, and America thanks you.

 VISIT

www.uso.org
www.treatsfortroops.com
www.anysoldier.com
www.penpalsforsoldiers.org
www.mysoldier.com

91. Take a Road Trip

America is *huge*! Seriously, we forget sometimes, but it's really gigantic and filled with some of the most spectacular places on earth. Just ask the president, who probably saw most of it on the campaign trail leading up to election day. But don't take our word for it—go see it for yourselves. Why not experience the diversity, complexity, and vastness of this great country of ours firsthand? Sure, you could fly from place to place, but why not go big? There's nothing like a road trip with friends. So recruit some of your closest BFFs, hit the road, and go explore the different nooks and crannies of America: stand in Times Square and gawk at the lights, have a drink on Bourbon Street, go for a jog on a California beach, or gaze into that giant rip in the earth called the Grand Canyon. You're sure to be surprised and amazed at what you'll find. But don't forget we're trying to be green these days, so do some research and see if you can outfit a car so that it runs on used vegetable oil before you go. Sound crazy? It's possible! While you won't be able to use any gas stations to fill up your tank along the way, vegetable oil has been shown to be a safe and efficient alternate fuel source. Just don't let any french fries make it into your gas tank or your road trip might end sooner than you expected. Happy trails, y'all!

 VISIT

www.roadtripamerica.com
www.roadtripusa.com
www.vegetableoilroadtrip.com (a cool blog which documents such a feat)
www.greasecar.com (information and products on how to convert your car to run on vegetable oil)

READ

On the Road by Jack Kerouac (See how the Beat Generation did it back in the day.)

92. Take a Socially Responsible Vacation

Sure, wet T-shirt contests are great. Who doesn't love a gallon of margarita for breakfast? But let's face it, spring break's fun lasts only as long as the hangover it gives you the next day. Want to see America and feel good about it afterwards? Then maybe you should consider going somewhere on a volunteer vacation. It's not only an inexpensive way to see parts of the country you've never been before, but it gives you the invaluable experience of being able to actually immerse yourself in a new town or city rather than being a tourist.

Want to get some calluses on those iPhone fingers? Habitat for Humanity has a "Global Village" program where volunteers get to work alongside U.S. families facing housing needs (remember Katrina?), building homes and bridges all across the country.

Love the environment and need to spend a week or two outside? **Earthwatch.org** has a ton of trips, which they call "Expeditions," where you get to work with leading environmental researchers on anything from studying caterpillars in Arizona to trying to see what effects climate change is having on wildlife to working with archeologists in South Dakota studying ancients ruins from our fore-foreforefathers.

Can't stop walking? Lucky you, Forrest Gump! Turns out the American Hiking Association has a ton of programs where you help clean trails while you're using them. Tighten those hiking boots and walk on over to **americanhiking.org** for more information.

And for those of you who want to sharpen those foreign language skills, why not take a volunteer vacation abroad? **Globalvolunteers.org** has plenty of trips listed by month so you can choose to take your vacay any time of the year. Tell HR you're out of there and hitting the road to go help the world and see if they don't cave in and give you a few extra days off next year. You never know!

So next time you find yourself with a week's worth of vacation, don't be so quick to book that trip to Cabo San Barfo; try something a bit more meaningful. America will thank you.

VISIT

www.earthwatch.org
www.americanhiking.org
www.globalvolunteers.org
www.habitat.org

93. Protect Our National Parks

From Glacier Bay in Alaska on the far West to Florida's Everglades Park on the East, this big ol' US of A of ours sure has some incredible places to visit. Talk about diversity. From mountains and streams to ice caps and oceans, we're talking some pretty breathtaking wonders, folks. And the beauty is, every time you have the opportunity to experience one of these places, you'll look through priceless windows into our past both historically and environmentally. These places make a home for so many plants and animals and offer awe-inspiring photo ops, all while providing a sanctuary for every single person who takes the time to visit them. Wow!

So what's the problem with that? Well, where nature lies so do natural resources like oil and petroleum. And unfortunately those are resources that our society still pretty heavily relies on. And until we can convince all our friends in Hummers to start riding bicycles, it's our responsibility to protect these special places so our grand-kids can proudly put that "This car climbed the Grand Canyon" bumper sticker on their Toyota Priuses.

You may be thinking, "What could I possibly do to help?" Well, this is definitely one of those situations where we need to stand up loud and proud and remind Washington how much we love Bryce Canyon and Acadia National Park. So get on the Internet horn and align yourself with one of the many organizations fighting to keep our wild lands condo free. That will ensure that all future generations will get to take in the splendor that is our National Parks system. Sign their petitions so they can go on to Congress and show them how much we care. Get more info about ways you can help at **nps.gov/gettinginvolved**, where they list all sorts of volunteer and job opportunities so you can not only say you've visited Yellowstone, but you've punched the clock there too.

VISIT

www.conservationfund.org
www.npca.org
www.nationalparks.org
www.nps.gov/gettinginvolved

94. Become Your Own Think Tank

"I will open the doors for government and ask you to be involved in your own democracy again."
—President Barack Obama (October 29, 2008)

Ever wanted to add "think tank member" to your résumé? What's a think tank you say? It's a fancy word, or should we say words, for a group of people who come together to solve problems. Well, you're a person who *obviously* has great ideas; you're reading this book after all, and so we think you should start writing down those flashes of genius and get ready to make the world a better place! Thanks to the folks at the Global Ideas Bank who've created an online sounding board for all of those brilliant ideas of yours, you too can say you're a part of a think tank. What a concept. But wait, it gets even better. After you post your ideas, people vote and pick the ones that they think are the best, further making you feel like the rock star that you are when you make it to the top of the list. Think you've come up with a way to make plastic bags from recycled sneakers? Send it in. How about a way to make public transportation free for the world just by taxing companies for using excessive packaging on their products? Why not? You never know. One person's fleeting thought can sometimes be the spark that changes a whole collective way of life for the better. So start brainstorming people. Your planet needs you!

VISIT

www.globalideasbank.org

95. Be Your Company's Conscience

Enron. Adelphia. Tyco. The corporate scandals that have rocked the headlines over the past years have given the public a good reason to look at corporate America with a healthy dose of skepticism. We're all for that, but we also think that companies can do a lot of good too. Corporate Social Responsibility (CSR) is a big buzzword these days, as corporations look to do better business by doing good. Sure, CSR might be a PR angle on a certain level, but if a company can take up the mantle of a good and worthy cause and champion it among the masses, well then who's going to complain if they get a little positive press for it? Regardless of what it is your company does, there's always a way it can give back to the community. Talk to your company's human resources department to learn more about what your company does in this area, and if they don't currently have any CSR projects, perhaps you might be the one to kick things off for them. Here are a couple of things you can check for:

- Charitable matching gifts. See if your company will match your donation to a charity of your choice, essentially doubling your contribution.
- Sponsorships. See if your company sponsors local charities or organizations, and ask how you can act as a company representative at events.
- Volunteer opportunities. See if your company does any volunteer work in the community, and if so, how you can get involved.

Remember, these initiatives aren't just for show; they fulfill a business objective, too. By implementing CSR campaigns, your company will not only seem more like a part of the community, but it'll also be seen as a responsible business. This in turn garners good will amongst both its employees and its customers, and makes it a more attractive place to work. Helping the bottom line and the community at the same time? Who's gonna argue with that?

96. Help Fight Cancer

Cancer sucks. That's all there is to say. And yes, we know that that's the understatement of the year, but it's so true. It's affecting more and more of our mothers, fathers, brothers, sisters, friends, and lovers every day. Chances are that every single one of us has had a loved one who has been affected by this devastating disease, and we must find a cure. Now. There are many things you can do to help, from running a 5K for research to buying a pink ribbon–endorsed blender the next time you've got a hankering to make smoothies to wearing the yellow wristband. And on an individual level, each of us should make sure that we perform routine checkups and screenings at the doctor's office and on our own for anything that seems out of the ordinary. Let's work together to make cancer the polio of our generation. In other words, history.

VISIT

www.cancer.org
www.livestrong.org
ww5.komen.org
www.standup2cancer.org

97. Cut Your Hair

Change is good, especially if it means you'll be helping someone else. Next time you're thinking about getting that post break-up haircut, why not donate your hair to a worthy cause? Be it children who are born with conditions such as alopecia or women who are suffering hair loss during chemotherapy, losing one's hair is an emotionally harrowing experience, and by donating your hair you'll be giving someone the gift of confidence, which truly is priceless. There are a few specifications for donations, which vary from charity to charity, so make sure you do your research before you go for the lop off. Here are a few rough guidelines to get you started:

- Hair must be clean and dry—no gray or chemically processed hair (sorry Britney).
- Put hair in a ponytail at the nape of your neck.
- You must have at least 8 to 10 inches of hair from tip to tip.
- Cut the hair above the rubber band.
- Wavy hair is accepted. Straighten it out to measure for the 8 inches.

Hey guys, don't think you're off the hook on this one. Consider saying adios to that *Lord of the Rings* flowing mane and help someone feel better about how they look. All of your lady friends will thank you for going all McDreamy. This means you, Kid Rock.

Need more information? Check out these links to get you started.

 **VISIT**

www.locksoflove.org
www.beautifullengths.com
www.squidoo.com/donateyourhair

98. Teach

"We can stop talking about how great teachers are and start rewarding them for their greatness."
—President Barack Obama (January 8, 2008)

Let's face it: the American educational system is broken, and we need your help to fix it. Not to get all Debbie Downer on you guys, but our schools are falling apart, the dropout rate is sky high, and kids in other countries are consistently outranking us on test scores. That's why the Obama administration has made it such a priority to get more qualified teachers into the classroom to help solve this problem. And that's where you come in to save the day, super person! Why not consider becoming a teacher? Teachers come into our lives at a time when all of us are the most vulnerable, and throughout our educational years they help shape us into the rock stars that we are today. And for that we owe them all an incredible debt of gratitude. Teaching may not bring you the wealth of being a banker or the prestige of being a doctor, but it will give you the satisfaction of knowing you're directly affecting the lives of kids. And not only that, but you'll be able to rest at night knowing that you are helping the future of this country get a leg up on the competition. Without teachers, none of us would be anything, and society needs to give them the respect that they deserve. We need more teachers who are passionate about the future of this country, and who are willing to go above and beyond what is needed to help educate the youth of America. Think you've got what it takes? Then get ready to get your classroom groove on and check out the Web sites below.

VISIT

www.teachforamerica.org (to see where teachers are needed most and how you can get started)
www.nyctf.org (to see how you can become a teacher in New York City, the nation's largest school system)

READ

Teacher Man by Frank McCourt

WATCH

The film *Freedom Writers* (2007) starring Hilary Swank

The film *Stand and Deliver* (1989) starring Edward James Olmos

99–108. Quickies. Change in 30 Seconds or Less!

Here are a few things to do that are so easy you might start doing them everyday! Or at least more often than never.

99. Hug it out.

100. Pick up a piece of random trash on the street. Throw it away.

101. Smell a flower and let it stay planted. No picking!

102. Buy a rechargeable battery.

103. Say hello to your neighbor.

104. Tell someone "I love you."

105. Use your turn signal.

106. Find an old friend who you've been thinking about on Facebook and reconnect.

107. Then pick up the phone and ask that old friend to lunch.

108. Show your grandma how to text.

SECTION III
Change Our World

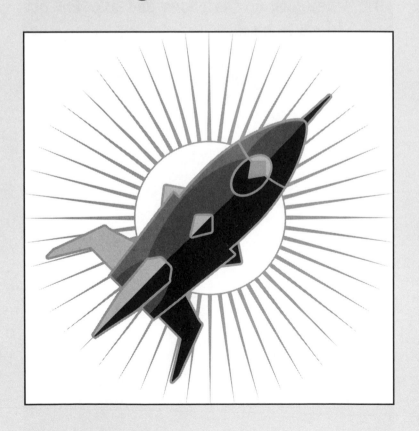

"Making your mark on the world is hard. If it were easy, everybody would do it. But it's not. It takes patience, it takes commitment, and it comes with plenty of failure along the way. The real test is not whether you avoid this failure, because you won't. It's whether you let it harden or shame you into inaction, or whether you learn from it; whether you choose to persevere."
—President Barack Obama (July 12, 2006)

Changing the world seems like a pretty big task. Because, well, it is. But it's also possible folks, have no doubt about that. Now, you might be wondering, "What can I really do while living here in (insert your hometown)-ville USA that will make a difference in the world?" The answer: plenty. And it's really not as hard as you might think. In fact, it might be a simple matter of tweaking your habits just a tiny bit. We don't all have to travel to the ends of the earth to do something to help change it. With today's technology, you can do it with a few clicks of your mouse from the comfort of your living room. Want to learn more? Of course you do! Some of the answers lie just beyond the period at the end of this sentence.

CHAPTER 7

EXTREME POVERTY

"Now the world will watch and remember what we do here—what we do with this moment. . . . Will we lift the child in Bangladesh from poverty, shelter the refugee in Chad, and banish the scourge of AIDS in our time?"
—President Barack Obama (July 24, 2008)

109. Fight the HIV/AIDS Pandemic

During the '80s and early '90s, AIDS was always in the national spotlight, thanks largely to vocal activists,

HIV/AIDS organizations, and a few dedicated celebrities. Then sometime during the late '90s, AIDS disappeared from the headlines, but AIDS never went away. In fact, it's now more deadly than ever. While we in America are lucky enough to have access to some of the best doctors and medicine in the world, not everyone is so fortunate. Today, there are over 30 million people living with HIV/AIDS around the world, with over 20 million of them living in sub-Saharan Africa. Roughly 2 million people die each year from AIDS, including more than 300,000 children, all because they don't have access to the same treatment that we have here. The sheer number of people infected is impossible to grasp, and it's enough to feel overwhelmed. But there is hope. Incredible organizations like the Global Fund are working across the board with governments, corporations, and people like you to provide education and medicine to help stop this modern day scourge. So how can you help with this seemingly endless problem? For starters, check out the following Web sites to learn about what these organizations are doing and see how you can support their efforts to stop this global pandemic both here at home and abroad. Then consider a few of these simple ways of supporting the cause:

- Wear a red ribbon to promote AIDS awareness.
- Participate in a fund-raiser, like an AIDS walk, ride, or a benefit concert.

- Buy Product (Red) items or support other similar campaigns where a portion of the funds from your purchase goes to help fight the AIDS pandemic.

VISIT

www.theglobalfund.org
www.theglobalfight.org
www.gatesfoundation.org
www.clintonfoundation.org
www.youthaids.org

110. Become an Ambassador for Africa

Bono called. And he wants you to know that Africa still needs you. You're not off the hook just because you bought that "USA for Africa" single off iTunes. Africa has more countries than any other continent that suffer from extreme third-world debt, which can lead to issues like starvation, poverty, and disease. The problem is that every country's failure to cancel their debts leaves them with little to no money to help their citizens, thus leaving millions in poverty. Unfortunately, 7 million children die each year as a result of conditions caused by the debt crisis. We know. Total downer. But we'll stop being all Sally Struthers now cause that's only one side of the coin, the bad news. The good news is that you can help.

The One Campaign is an organization with more than 2 million members who are committed to the fight against poverty and preventable diseases, particularly in Africa. It was cofounded by that U2 front man we mentioned earlier, and its whole mission is to try to get money and programs together to help Africa by working directly with policy makers in Washington. We know, policy sounds confusing, but here's where you come in.

Because they're primarily an advocacy organization, they need you to raise your voice and spread their message. In other words, One wants you to become an Ambassador for Africa. Next stop: the UN, you Ambassador you! How does one make their cause known in this big old sea of problems you may ask? Start by calling your Congressman, or by writing a letter to your local newspaper's editor telling them you think the United States should be helping the people in Africa more—the more attention you can get, the better. That will only help the people at One get their issues at the top of every policy maker's list. Top of the list means more money, more programs, more action, more change. So get ready to be heard. Better start warming up those inner activist muscles; you'll need 'em.

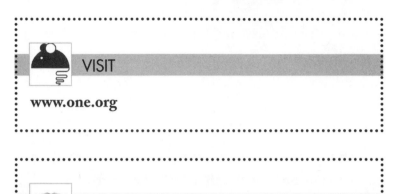

VISIT

www.one.org

READ

The End of Poverty by Jeffrey Sachs

111. Champion Clean Water

It's kind of crazy the things we take for granted living in the United States. Most of us don't pause to think when we turn on the faucet for a glass of water. But you'll pause next time when you consider that one billion people on the planet don't have access to safe drinking water. What? You heard us. One billion. That's like 1 out of every 6 people on the planet, just so you get a scope of how many people don't have this basic necessity. People, especially women and children, spend hours each day going out to fetch water from wells so they can have something to drink, and many times this water isn't even clean. Why is clean water so important? The fact is that unsafe drinking water and lack of basic sanitation are responsible for 80 percent of sicknesses in developing countries and kill millions of people annually. Think of that the next time you complain when the hot water in your shower goes out and maybe you won't be so upset. But there are great organizations out there that are working to rectify this startling statistic. And they need your help. Here are a few tips to get you started:

- Learn more about water issues that are currently affecting such a huge part of the global population.
- Sign up for e-mail blasts or join a group on Facebook for updates about what's going on around this issue.
- Raise funds for organizations that drill wells for local communities.
- Spread the word and get your community, friends, coworkers, classmates, or congregation involved in this issue.
- Volunteer your time to help organizations to work on the ground.

 VISIT

www.wateradvocates.org
www.charitywater.org
www.globalwater.org

112. Feed the World

Looking around at our fellow Americans and their desire to battle the bulge, it's hard to imagine that there are still people who don't get enough food to eat these days. But unfortunately this is a very painful reality that affects so many living around the world today. Consider these statistics: more than 920 million people across the world go hungry, including more than 35 million people here in the United States alone. And every 5 seconds, a child will die from hunger-related causes somewhere in the world. And while we've all been suffering through the recession, we still have it very good compared to the 1.4 billion people in the world who earn less than a $1.25 per day. Just because we don't hear any more songs such as "We Are the World" or "Do They Know It's Christmas?" like we did in the '80s doesn't mean this issue went away. Not in the least. We shouldn't feel guilty because of these numbers, but it's important to know these things so that we recognize how fortunate most of us are here in America. Facts like these will remind you to clean your plate when you can, and make sure to take a to-go bag with you from restaurants so that you're not wasting food. So join up and learn more about this issue through one of these organizations today and help make world hunger a thing of the past.

VISIT

www.whyhunger.org
www.care.org
www.fao.org

113. Join the Peace Corps

Back in the day, this is where it all started. President Kennedy spoke these fateful words on his inauguration day in 1961, "Ask not what your country can do for you—ask what you can do for your country," and ushered in a new era of service for this nation. And today, President Obama is echoing those same sentiments with his words and his actions. But throughout those years in between, there is one organization that has kept that torch of American service lit: the Peace Corps. It's still very much alive and kicking and continues to better the lives of people across the world through the hard work of Americans like you. With a slogan like "The Toughest Job You'll Ever Love," you know you'll be testing your limits, but talk about getting a chance to change your perspective of how you view the world. Just because you're not part of the Flower Power generation doesn't mean you can't give back the same way they did; the Peace Corps still sends volunteers to work in 74 countries across the world in all sorts of jobs, including community development, the environment, and education. You might be in a classroom somewhere teaching English, or working directly with at-risk youth to develop their leadership skills, or be an advocate and educator on HIV/AIDS prevention and care. There's no limit to what you might achieve. So if you've ever wanted to change the world, joining the Peace Corps might be an option for you. Not only will it teach you about the world, but more importantly, it'll teach you about yourself.

 VISIT

www.peacecorps.gov

CHAPTER 8

HUMAN RIGHTS

"Will we stand for the human rights of the dissident in Burma, the blogger in Iran, or the voter in Zimbabwe?"
—President Barack Obama (July 24, 2008)

114. Help Human Rights in Darfur and Beyond

Ever hear of Darfur? Sure you have; who hasn't these days? Because when George Clooney talks, we all listen.

It's horrible what's going on over there, but the good news is that at least the public is becoming more aware of this terrible situation. And with awareness comes action. Unfortunately, there are other human rights catastrophes going on around the world that most people have never even heard of. Like the situation in D.R. Congo. *Um, where?* Or the oppression in Burma. *Um, what?* Yeah, don't let those always be your answers when it comes to world issues. Living the good life here in America should mean that we take advantage of our situation to help others as often as we can. Sure, we know that it's difficult to follow the events in every corner of the world, but it's always a good idea to at least have some notion or passing knowledge as to what's going on elsewhere beyond our borders. And at the very least, learning about these situations shows us how good we really have it here at home. There are plenty of incredible international organizations with boots on the ground that help to monitor human rights abuses worldwide and bring attention to these issues. And while traveling to the dangerous hot spots of the world probably isn't everyone's cup of tea, there are still lots of other ways that you can get involved.

- Consider donating to, fund-raising for, or joining a human rights organization.

- Learn about the various campaigns that each organization works on worldwide and see if one speaks directly to you. Then become invested in that specific cause, learn more about it, and get involved.
- Attend events and speak with representatives to find out what else you can do.

 VISIT

www.savedarfur.org
www.hrw.org
www.mercycorps.org
www.amnesty.org
www.oxfam.org

115. Beware of Bad Bling

Diamonds. They're a girl and a guy's best friend. But not everyone realizes that those shiny little rocks can come with a steep price. The diamond trade has a brutal history and legacy, one that has fueled wars, (like the one in Sierra Leone) decimated countries, left countless numbers dead and maimed, and forced innocent children into becoming soldiers. But you don't have to feel guilty about wanting the finer things in life; you should just make sure that the diamonds that you purchase are not "conflict" or "blood" diamonds, ones that have been used to help fuel conflicts. You can do this by making sure your diamonds have gone through the Kimberley Process Certification Scheme, an initiative that regulates the trade of rough diamonds in the world with the objective of keeping "conflict diamonds" out from the marketplace. It's up to all of us as consumers to try to buy diamonds from reputable dealers who can vouch for where their diamonds come from. Hey, if you're shelling out that much money, you should feel free to ask as many questions as you like, right? So ask away!

 VISIT

www.kimberleyprocess.com (Check out the FAQs section.)

www.un.org/peace/africa/Diamond

 **WATCH**

The film *Blood Diamond* (2006) starring Leo DiCaprio doing an awesome accent

116. Give Peace a Chance

Unfortunately, around the world, there are too many people who look at each other as enemies. But really, aren't people just people the world over, and everyone basically wants the same thing: a safe home for their family, a job to put some money in their pocket, and a future that's brighter than the present? It's all the other stuff that seems to get in the way. Thankfully other people see things the same way we do and are doing something about it. Seeds of Peace is a great program that brings together young people from different regions of conflict across the world to a camp in Maine to give them the leadership skills needed for conflict resolution, reconciliation, and co-existence. Since 1993, thousands of teens from the Middle East, South Asia, and the Balkans have participated in this program, giving hope that these hot spots of conflict might not always have to be so hot in the future. PeacePlayers International is another organization with similar goals, only using the game of basketball as a way to bridge social divides between youth. Hey, you gotta figure if you can shoot hoops with someone, then they can't be that bad, right? Check out these two programs and see what you can do get involved. Peace out, yo!

VISIT

www.seedsofpeace.org
www.peaceplayersintl.org

117. Support Refugees

Imagine that you're at home, minding your own business, when all of a sudden through no fault of your own, you're forced to leave all that you know and that is familiar behind, not knowing where you are going or if you will return. Yeah, we'd be pretty pissed too. Now consider this: more than 40 million people worldwide have been forced from their homes because of conflict or persecution like in Iraq or the Sudan. That's like evicting all of Canada and then some. Well, that's the current state of refugees in the world today. And not only that, but it's estimated that 50 percent of them are kids. At best, many live in huge camps with thousands, even millions of others, just waiting until it's safe to return to their homes. But that might never happen. Talk about a sad situation all around. But as always, there are good people out there, just like yourself, who are working hard on this issue, trying to make sure these people eventually have a home. Here's how you can help:

- Become educated on the plights of various refugees across the world.
- Write letters or sign petitions urging politicians to take action on different issues affecting refugees.
- Support an organization that is working on these issues and help spread awareness.
- Consider working with a local community-based organization that is helping refugees who are settling in your area get accustomed to life in the United States.

 VISIT

www.refugees.org
www.refugeesinternational.org
www.unhcr.org

READ

What Is the What by Dave Eggers

---

118. Say "Later" to Land Mines

Chances are that when you step out the door in the morning you have a lot on your mind. Will I be late for work? Will my crush ever call me back? Am I going to step on a land mine today? *Huh?* Yeah, probably not that last one. While the world's armies have used land mines for centuries during times of war, most armies don't play nice and clean up after themselves. As is the case with most wars, it's the innocent that usually end up paying the price. Land mines are unfortunately part of the landscape of many countries including Afghanistan, Cambodia, Croatia, Ethiopia, and Nepal to name a few, and UNICEF estimates that 30 to 40 percent of all land mine victims are children under the age of 15. As Americans, it's pretty crazy to learn that there are between 70 and 80 million undetonated landmines in a third of the world's countries. These kill or maim as many as 20,000 civilians each year. Why so many? Because they are extremely cheap to make but very expensive to remove.

And they don't get old either—World War II mines are still killing people. Yeah, it's a pretty frightening thought.

But don't worry, it's not all doom and gloom. Progress is being made, and the number of active mines out there is decreasing. You may be asking yourself, *What can I possibly do to help?* The first thing you should do is call Congress and urge U.S. participation in the international treaty to ban cluster bombs. More bombs mean more mines that need to be deactivated.

Looking to do more? Why not get a group together and adopt a minefield? Adopt-a-Minefield is a campaign of the United Nations Association of the United States— and all the money raised goes toward helping to save lives through mine clearance, mine risk education, and survivor assistance. Help make landmines a thing of the past. Now if we could only put an end to the whole idea of war . . . and give peace a chance.

CALL

Capitol Switchboard (202) 224-3121

VISIT

www.landmines.org

119. Respect the Ladies and Support Women's Rights

When we hear about how women are treated in some other countries, it makes us cringe. It's a sad truth, but 1 out of every 3 women worldwide is beaten or abused at some point in her life. For years under the Taliban in Afghanistan, women weren't allowed to leave the house unless they were fully covered from head to toe in a burqa. Holy crap, we think that's nuts. And wrong. Where are all the Susan B. Anthony's of the world when we need them to help give women equal rights? There are all kinds of issues that women are facing across the world, most of which are entirely regionally and culturally specific. So if you want to stand up for our mothers, sisters, and daughters everywhere, the first step is to learn what is going on and where, and what can be done about it. Like the Queen of Soul Aretha Franklin sang, all we're asking is for a little R-E-S-P-E-C-T!

VISIT

www.amnestyusa.org (Select the Violence Against Women section.)
www.unifem.org

 READ

A Thousand Splendid Suns by Khaled Hosseini to get a sense of what women went through under the Taliban.

CHAPTER 9

WE ARE THE WORLD

"The burdens of global citizenship continue to bind us together. . . . Partnership and cooperation among nations is not a choice, it is the one way, the only way, to protect our common security and advance our common humanity."
—President Barack Obama (July 24, 2008)

120. Support a Budding Business

In these days of online social networks, the phrase "six degrees of separation" seems to ring true more and more.

With sites like Facebook, the world is getting even more connected, and it's so much easier for us to connect with people around the world. Go ahead and check your friends list—chances are that a few of those peeps are living outside of your state at least. In that same way, it's also becoming easier for us to make a difference in the lives of others. For the price of a cheap night out with friends, you can go online and loan someone half a world away a few bucks to get their fledgling business off the ground. It's a cool little concept called microfinance, and it's all the rage these days. For a lot of people who live in poverty, a small business is the only way to get ahead in life. But since they don't have any funds or assets, it's very hard for them to get credit or loans from a traditional bank to start their business venture. That's where you come in. Microfinancing lets you help a struggling entrepreneur somewhere by giving them a small loan (as little as $25) that you will eventually get back. It's a pretty cool way to help someone across the world build a better life for themselves. Think of it as social networking for good. So how about holding off on those last few pitchers of beer and loaning that money instead? Who knows, you could be helping the next Apple, Nike, or Google get off the ground. Plus the universe (and your liver) will thank you.

VISIT

www.kiva.org

READ

Banker to the Poor by Nobel Prize winner Muhammad Yunas

---

121. Travel the World

You're young. You've got your whole life in front of you. Why not pull out that passport and start packing? There is no better way to open your eyes to the world around you than by traveling, which is way different from a vacation. Vacations center around staying still, while travel is all about moving around and seeing new things. Vacations have lounge chairs on the beach; travel has bumpy twelve-hour bus rides through the mountains of Peru. A vacation will get you tan, which will fade faster than you can say "wish you were here," while traveling gives you an experience that will stay with you forever.

Taking time off and going someplace new can be scary, especially in this day and age where we're told we need to get out there and get jobs and have careers and start families. There hardly seems like there's enough time to live life, let alone take off for a few weeks to travel. But here's the deal: the older you get, the harder it is to unplug from the world you live in and hit the road, backpack in tow. The excuses pile up: the mortgage has to be paid; the kids have to go to school; the job needs to be done. The time is now to hit the road of life and experience new places. Don't wait until you've retired, cause how fun will it really be climbing Machu Picchu with a walker?

So let's say you find yourself with a little time to travel and can't figure out how to take the next step. We've got some ways for you to get packing in no time. First things first. You're going to need a passport. Make sure to smile at the camera knowing they'll inevitably find the most unflattering angle possible. Do you know anyone who actually has a good passport pic? Neither do we. Keep our postal service working through rain, sleet, and snow and get your ticket to ride at the post office. You can find more info at their Web site.

Need help planning? So many places to see! So many things to do! How does one plan this sort of adventure?

Bootsnall.com has an awesome round the world trip planner and **independenttraveler.com** has tons of invaluable tips and tricks for making your trip smooth sailing. And if you decide to really go for that circumnavigation sort of trip, check out a travel broker like Star Alliance or One World. By going through a broker, you're sure to get not only a good cost, but they'll also help keep you moving in one direction so you don't have to back track, which will ultimately make your carbon footprint lighter. Help the planet and get that passport filled with stamps why don't ya?

And as for accommodation, why not find a place to crash for free and meet some new people while you're at it? **Couchsurfing.com** is devoted to just that! Did you say free? That's right. Shut those wallets. It's a great idea that uses that age-old practice of the couch surf. If that concept brings up one too many memories of back-breaking futons, try to think of it as a place to find international homestays where you get to stay at someone's house and learn more about the community they live in at no cost. Someone stop the presses. This is genius!

And what about your place, while you're gone? Why not trade digs with some other fellow traveler while you're seeing the world? Someone in France gets to live in your sweet pad in Brooklyn, and you get to see the Louvre every morning when you wake up. And this way you know someone will be watering your plants while you're away. Winner! Check out **homeexchange.com** for more information.

 VISIT

www.usps.com/passport
www.bootsnall.com
www.independenttraveler.com
www.couchsurfing.com
www.homeexchange.com
www.staralliance.com
www.oneworld.com

 READ

The Practical Nomad: How to Travel around the World by Edward Hasbrouck
Around the World in 80 Days by Jules Verne
1,000 Places to See Before You Die: A Traveler's Life List by Patricia Schultz
Make the Most of Your Time on Earth by Rough Guides

WATCH

The reality show *The Amazing Race*

122. Learn a Foreign Language

Hola. Bonjour. Ciào. Góðan dag. Mambo. Now that we've got the greetings over with, let's move onto some real conversation. What? The buck stops at hello? Well then it's time to call Berlitz and learn what comes after "I'm fine. How are you?" Our world is a veritable melting pot of different cultures, people, and, yes, languages. And we're not saying you have to become fluent in the entire UN, only suggesting adding the ability to have a conversation, even a basic one, in a language other than English, would be a great little tool to have in the toolbox called you.

If you're scared at the idea of going back to Madame Tafoya's tenth-grade French classroom, fear not; there are many ways to pick up the foreign gift of gab without even setting foot in a school. From books on tape (or should we say MP3s on your iPod?) to joining a group in your hometown with other people who're trying to sharpen their mastery of Bulgarian, you'll be shocked at how easy it is to learn a new language these days. Luckily for all you weary Google searchers, **elanguageschool.net** has compiled listings of Web sites where you can often download lessons to help you on your quest to learn a new language for absolutely free. Having trouble figuring out how to say in Dutch, "Where is the recycling center?" Head over to **babelfish.yahoo.com** where you can type in what you're trying to say and it'll convert it for you (it's "waar het recyclerende centrum is" by the way).

How bout this for fun? Why don't you rent your favorite film and watch it in German with the subtitles off? Or turn on Telemundo next Saturday and sit back and relax and take in a few telenovelas for the day? You'll be talking the talk in no time at all.

 VISIT

www.elanguageschool.net
babelfish.yahoo.com

123. Invest Responsibly

Okay, we know, we know. A penny saved is a penny earned. But how does one save for your future *and* invest one's money in a socially responsible way? We know we want to be able to retire and head on down to Florida with all of our other friends when we're sixty-five. And of course we want to have some golden years where we take that luxury cruise around the world all the while knowing we won't have to eat cat food when we get home. So is there a way to save for all that, but by helping others? The answer is yes, and luckily there are quite a few companies out there that believe in the earning power of investing in the world, and they want to help you do it. Check out any of the Web sites below to get more information about ways to invest in a socially responsible way. Or talk to your financial planner and tell her you want to diversify your options. And by "diversify" we mean helping to make the world a better place. Jackpot!

 VISIT

www.domini.com
www.socialfunds.com
www.socialinvest.org

READ

Investing for Change: Profit from Responsible Investment by Augustin Lander and Vinay Nair to get a sense of the economics of how social investing actually work.

124–130 BUY BUY BUY!

Okay, we've been telling you to stop spending your money on junk you don't need, but now it's time to open those wallets and start spending responsibly! There are many ways to use your benjamins to not only get some cool stuff, but to help the world too. Here are just a few of the many ways to put those dollars to work in a socially positive way:

124. Buy a Malaria Net

Nothing But Nets is an organization that was started by *Sports Illustrated*'s Rick Reilly and the UN Foundation. The idea is simple: Spend ten bucks and help stop the spread of malaria in Africa, which is rapidly becoming one of the most deadly diseases on the planet.

Oh, you don't know how malaria is spread? Ever hear that annoying buzzing in your ear that makes you start swatting feverishly? Mr. Mosquito? Yes that's right, those pesky mosquitoes aren't just loud and bloodthirsty, they're deadly too. And if you live in Africa, the best way to stop them is to cover your bed with a net so they don't bite you and give you malaria when you're sleeping. Sports use nets. Bed nets save lives. See the connection? One bed net can safely last a family for about four years, a pretty incredible rate of return. According to NBN's Web site, "Studies show that use of insecticide-treated bed nets can reduce transmission as much as 90 percent in areas with high coverage rates." So head on over to Nothing But Nets and pull out a ten spot and go save some lives! It's that simple.

 VISIT

www.nothingbutnets.net

125. Buy a Goat. A Flock of Chicks. A Farm!

Heifer International's goal is to help people around the world obtain a sustainable source of food and income. How do they do that? By creating an online gift catalog, which makes it easy to spend your money wisely. The way it works is you make a "donation" of livestock, be it one goat, a herd of sheep, or whatever you can afford. Recipients agree to share the offspring of gift animals with others in need in their community, making them equal partners in the fight to end world hunger. What an awesome example of how the trickle down theory can be benevolent! And your gift doesn't stop there! By giving, you'll also be helping children and families around the world receive training that will further help them become more self-reliant. Win. Win. So in other words, by purchasing through Heifer you're giving the gift to help end world hunger and poverty. *Baaaa*. Sure beats an iTunes gift certificate.

VISIT

www.heifer.org

126. Get Your Pro-Social Etsy Fix!

Spend your money in a socially responsible way and buy a rural artisan's craft. From bedding and pillows to oven mitts, Tiolonia is a nonprofit organization selling crafts from the Barefoot College in Tilonia, Rajasthan, India. All money from sales goes toward addressing the basic needs of the rural poor: water, health, education, energy, and employment. This is a great organization with even better products. Can't decide what country you want to buy in? Then Ten Thousand Villages is the place for you. They've created an online mall featuring fair trade hand-made goods from thirty-eight countries all over the globe. And we all know fair trade lets artisans earn a fair wage for everything they make, so these gifts aren't just cool, they're socially responsible as well.

 VISIT

www.tilonia.org
www.tenthousandvillages.com

127. Purchase More Product (RED)

Product (RED) is an organization started by—yes you guessed it—Bono, created to work with The Global Fund to help stop HIV/AIDS in Africa. The way it works is simple: buy something that's been made (RED), such as select iPods, Converse, and Dell products, and a percentage of the price tag goes directly to help saving lives. As of Spring 2009, the amount of money generated by you buying (RED) products has helped give 825,000 people with HIV lifesaving antiretroviral therapy for a whole year. Nice.

VISIT

www.joinred.com

128. Pay Junk Mail to Go Away. Forever.

Around 100 million trees and 28 billion gallons of water are used to send junk mail to Americans every year, according to **greendimes.com.** You can stop 75 percent of unsolicited mail by registering on the Mail Preference Service on the Direct Marketing Association Web site. Within 90 days, most unsolicited mail will stop. Or if you want to go all out, for $20 Mailstopper will not only stop 90 percent of those crappy catalogs from coming to your house, but they'll even plant a tree for you! Seriously, what would you rather have? Another catalog for some weird fruit of the month club or a whole fruit tree planted courtesy of you? But wait, there's more! Check out **41pounds.org.** It's similar to Mailstopper, but they offer a five-year ban on crap mail for only $41. Now that's some change we can totally believe in.

VISIT

www.greendimes.com

> www.41pounds.org
> www.the-dma.org

129. Buy a $199 Laptop and Help a Child Get Online

Give a child in a developing country the gift of connectivity, knowledge, and the opportunity of a lifetime. All for the low, low price of $199. That's right! Sounds crazy, right? Well let's say thanks to those geniuses at MIT who've figured out a way to make a technologically advanced computer that brings the power of the digital age to poorer countries and that's also affordable. The concept is simple: the more connected people are, the easier it is for them to have access to better education. The better the education, the more equipped they are to share their knowledge with others. It is a small world after all, especially with the help of a life-changing PC. So pull out those wallets and make a donation of a computer to a child in another country. And don't be surprised if they ask you to become their Facebook friend, too!

 VISIT

www.laptop.org

130. Buy Shoes. From Tom.

Tom's shoes are great. Not only are they super cute, but they're also inexpensive, good for the environment (some are vegan), and here's the best part of all: for every pair of shoes you buy, they'll give a pair to a child in need. So next time you find your feet yearning for some new kicks, pass by Payless and head online to Tom's. There's sure to be a color or style to fit your fashion sense, not to mention your conscience will be feeling great every time you hit the ground walking.

VISIT

www.tomsshoes.com

CHAPTER 10

ENVIRONMENT

"This is the moment when we must come together to save this planet. Let us resolve that we will not leave our children a world where the oceans rise and famine spreads and terrible storms devastate our lands."
—President Barack Obama (July 24, 2008)

131. Start a Compost Heap

Have some extra garbage on your hands? How about some soil, air, water, and time? If so, then you're all set to start a compost heap! What's compost you ask? It's organic material that, when broken down naturally over time, becomes healthy soil and can be used as plant fertilizer. Organic materials can mean anything from yard trimmings to egg shells to fruits to sawdust to food scraps. Who knew that our leftover garbage could be so useful? Sound complicated? It isn't really, but there are a few more details that you need to learn to get started, which can be found at the following Web sites. Remember, nature breaks these organic items down anyway, so all you gotta do is collect and separate them from the rest of your garbage, learn the proper steps needed to start a compost heap, and then start the fun. But remember to read up on the specific steps, or you might just end up with a stinking pile of garbage, which won't be helping anyone. And consider this: a lot of this organic waste now just goes into landfills and accounts for 24 percent of all garbage. So think of composting as nature's way of recycling, and by doing so you'll be helping to cut down on the size of your town dump. The next time you go to throw something organic out, consider putting it aside from the rest of your trash and throwing it into a compost heap. And besides, all that compost will come in handy when you are planting that garden we talked about earlier. Who knew that rotting and decaying waste could be so interesting?

VISIT

www.epa.gov (Do a search for "composting.")
www.vegweb.com/composting

 WATCH

The Pixar film *WALL-E* (2008). (There's no composting going on, but plenty of footage of giant landfills and a desolate, wasted earth. So it's a great film to get you motivated to start composting! Plus we just love this flick.)

132. Green Up Your House, a.k.a. Live Like Ed

We should all strive to live like Ed—Ed Begley Jr. that is. If you don't know Ed, then let us introduce you. He's an actor and activist who is the OG environmental crusader. In other words, he drove an electric car in the '80s, way before Leo made the Prius red carpet worthy. Bono is to

Africa what Ed Begley Jr. is to the environment. We know we don't all have the means to build a brand new sustainable apartment or house, but there are lower cost things you can do to make your home more Begley-ific. Here are a few tips to get you started:

- Call your landlord and ask him or her to get wind or solar power. More than half of all electricity consumers in the United States now have the option of purchasing green power from their utility provider, which you can find by visiting the Department of Energy's state-by-state list of providers. And if you're the homeowner, what are you waiting for? Go help the earth out will ya?
- Turn down that thermostat.
- Most households shell out 50 to 70 percent of their energy budgets on heating and cooling. For every degree you lower the thermostat, you'll save between 1 percent and 3 percent of your heating bill. *Guaranteed* to show you the money.
- Weatherproof your front door and windows. Most hardware stores have a wide array of inexpensive options that you should check out. Thanks to President Obama's new tax rebate, you can get money back for making your home more energy efficient. For example, homeowners who install certified energy-

efficient windows, furnaces, and air conditioners can qualify for a tax credit equal to 30 percent of their costs, up to a total of $1,500. Not bad for a day's work helping Mother Earth.

For more information, check out these Web sites that can help you navigate the tricky path toward ultimate greenness.

VISIT

www.energystar.gov (Find out more tips here.)
www.edbegley.com (See the master Mister Ed at work.)
www.energy.gov
www.treehugger.com (for a great all-around resource that can help you answer all those green questions keeping you up at night. You'll like what your newly tinted green eyes will see.)

133. Stop Feeding the Great Garbage Patch

Ever hear of the Great Pacific Garbage Patch? It's a swirling mass of millions of pounds of debris and plastic smack dab in the middle of the Pacific Ocean, taking up an area that's perhaps larger than the state of Texas. Yeah, we know, gross. If that doesn't freak you out, keep in mind that it's been building in size since the 1950s. It's filled with toys, shoes, bottles, bags, and other junk—you name it—from all over the world that has somehow ended up out to sea and accumulated in one area because of ocean currents. At places, this debris can be up to 90 feet deep. OMG! WTF? Exactly. All this swirling garbage is creating an ecological crisis, especially because plastic doesn't break down easily. Marine critters mistake the floating bits of plastic for food and eat them, and we don't need to depress you with the sad story about what happens next. Even Oprah is talking about the Garbage Patch, so you know it's serious. So what can you do about this? Well, it's not an easy fix for sure, but since plastic is the worst offender, it's all about cutting down on your consumption. Remember these tips:

- Reduce, Reuse, Recycle. Better get used to hearing that.
- Cut down on using plastic bags. C'mon, do you really need an entire plastic bag for that candy bar? That's what pockets are for. And how hard is it to schlep a canvas tote bag to the grocery store? Answer: not very. Do you really want ten more plastic bags worth of groceries cluttering up your home anyways?

- Making a choice between items that come in glass or plastic? Choose glass.
- Put trash in its place. That means the garbage can. All that junk that you see lying in the street? It ends up going down the drain and into the sewer. And anyone who watched the Pixar flick *Finding Nemo* knows the answer to the next question: Where do a lot of sewer drains lead eventually? Yep, the ocean. Think about it.

Seventy percent of the earth is covered by ocean—that's a helluva lot. They're home to untold amounts of marine life, including our mysterious friend the Giant Squid, and we can't just look at them as our giant trash can. So do your best to keep our oceans free of debris and garbage, and support organizations like the Surfrider Foundation that are working toward this end. The oceans are a shared resource of all the people on this planet, and it's up to each of us to make sure they stay clean and healthy. As a Hawaiian native, we're sure the president agrees with that.

 VISIT

www.greatgarbagepatch.org
www.surfrider.org

134. Break the Plastic Water Bottle Habit

Here's a thought to stew on: More people in the United States buy bottled water than any other beverage around, with the exception of soft drinks. But we already have the luxury of turning on a faucet and clean, fresh, filtered water comes gushing out. So why then, if we have access to all the clean water that we want for free, would we spend our money to *buy* water in a bottle? It's called marketing, people! Don't be a sucker and shell out your hard-earned cash for something you can get for free. To drive the point home, there are studies out there that suggest some of the branded drinking water in bottles comes from the same sources as the water from your tap. Hmm . . . In addition, the jury's still out on whether or not drinking bottled water can have any negative health effects, because there are studies being done to see if chemicals from the plastic bottles can seep into the water itself over time. But okay, forget about saving some cash, and forget about any potential health hazards. Consider dropping your bottled water habit for Mother Earth. Think about where all those empty plastic bottles go: only about 13 percent of them get recycled, and the rest end up in landfills. And we're not even mentioning the other effects that all that fuel and energy spent shipping and transporting all these water bottles all over the world has on the environment. So how about we save a little cash and the earth at the same time and drink more water from the tap? If you have to, invest in a water filter and a little reusable container so you can take your clean tap water with you on the go. You save money, you're not thirsty, and you help save the earth too. Sounds like a win-win-win to us.

VISIT

www.nrdc.org/water/drinking/qbw.asp

135. Reuse and Restyle Your Clothing

Who says those purple culottes aren't cool anymore? One man's trash is another man's treasure, so next time you find you have a pair of pants that don't fit, don't throw them out—pay them forward. "Reduce, reuse, and recycle" is a mantra that can be taken across all arenas of our lives, even clothing. We love the idea behind Swaporamarama, an organization that sponsors events where people are encouraged to bring a bag of clothing that's passed their

personal wearability test. Sewing machines, embellishments, and professional sewing enthusiasts are on hand
to help you channel your inner Marc Jacobs. Can you say
fabulous? Soon you'll have saved the earth *and* gotten one
step closer to being on *Project Runway*—not bad for a
day's work.

If the idea of kicking it home-ec style makes you
cringe, feel free to donate your clothing to the Salvation
Army or a local homeless shelter in your neighborhood.
And in some cases, companies like Patagonia, Nike, and
Uniqlo will take back anything you've bought from them
free of charge. Through Patagonia's Common Threads
Garment Recycling Program, they'll turn your unusable
garments into new clothing. Who says a shirt can't experience reincarnation?

 VISIT

www.swaporamarama.org
www.salvationarmyusa.org
www.patagonia.com (Look under the
"Environmentalism" section.)

136. Eat Better Fish and Meat

Yum. Is that methylmercury with a touch of trenbolone acetate, melengestrol acetate, and zeranol I taste? I must have your recipe! Unfortunately, there's a lot of cause for concern these days regarding hormones and chemicals in farm-raised fish and genetically modified meat products. Not only are these ingredients adding to health risks such as cancer and the premature onset of puberty, but they're making the earth sick as well. According to the guru of the environment Al Gore, "If more Americans shifted to a less meat-intensive diet, we could greatly reduce CO2 emissions and also save vast quantities of water and other precious natural resources." Okay, we're not saying you have to say adios to fried chicken, we're just suggesting you know where your meat is coming from and what effects its production has on the earth. Farm-raised hormone-free beef is fine every once in a while, just don't forget about your old friend vegetables.

 VISIT

www.eatwild.com (Get your moo fix. But make it healthy.)

> **www.nrdc.org** (Search for "sushi guide." Watch out,
> sushi, we're watching you.)

137. Become a Citizen Scientist

Bored of that desk job? Tired of watching reruns of the PGA golf tour on Sunday afternoons? Why not work for the earth on your time off? Sure looks better on your resume than a high score on *Rock Band*. Citizen science is a term used to describe scientific projects that are worked on by average Joes, many of whom have no specific training. That means you too can wear a lab coat! Most projects involve basic tasks like counting and observing, which you don't need a PhD for. Not to mention it's a great way to get out of the house and meet other people who share your passion for doing good.

There are a ton of great programs out there to whet your inner science whistle. Love birds? Cornell University's Department of Ornithology has a great program in which you get to help tackle problems ranging from global warming to avian disease. Always wanted to go to space but never got around to filling out that pesky NASA job application you saw one night on monster.com? Check out **research.dynamicpatterns.com** where they list all kinds of activities ranging from counting stars to identifying galaxies. Houston, we have lift off! And if you're like us and you have too many interests to even know where to get started, check out **sas.org.** This is the only nonprofit dedicated to helping people take part in scientific adventures of all kinds. Now go get 'em, Professor!

VISIT

www.birds.cornell.edu
research.dynamicpatterns.com
www.sas.org

138. Help Keep the Wild Things Where They Are

If you haven't seen the image of a mother polar bear and her cub struggling to stay afloat on a tiny piece of ice, you must have just stepped out of a time capsule, so welcome to now. And the reality of now is that global warming and massive amounts of industrialization have destroyed the natural habitats of many of the world's wildlife. Unlike us loud and opinionated Homo sapiens, animals can't speak or else, trust us, they'd be screaming their guts out. We must save and protect not only the creatures on the endangered list, but all the others too. So all you amateur Dr. Dolittles of the world unite and start being the voice for all of the wonderful creatures, big and small, on this great big planet called earth. How to get started? Feeling overwhelmed by the fact that the planet is one big old place? Here are a few resources:

- **The Nature Conservancy,** since being founded in 1951, has saved more than 119 million acres of land and five thousand miles of rivers. They have tons of volunteer activities ranging from trail maintenance in Maine to leading nature walks in California. So get out there and help keep Mother Nature's house nice and lush so all those animals have a nice place to lie down at night after a hard day at the office.
- **The World Wildlife Fund** is pretty much the premiere nonprofit dedicated to saving and preventing the extinction of all the endangered species walking, flying, and swimming on our planet. So if helping animals is your thing, run—don't walk—to their Web site.
- Hey! Fish are people too! **The Ocean Conservancy** wants you to be a hero for the seven seas. From writing your congressperson to helping clean up the

ocean, there are tons of ways for all you fish lovers to get involved.

- And let's not forget about our friend, the poster child of global warming, the polar bear. We can't let this beautiful creature down. **The National Resources Defense Council (NRDC)** is fighting to save our friends in the Arctic and they need your help. Send a letter or e-mail to President Obama's interior secretary to rescue the polar bear, because we all know they can't wait any longer. You can get more info and watch videos on their Web site.

- While we're talking about watching videos, as an animal lover you must have seen *Planet Earth*. And if not, get online and put that baby in your Netflix queue. This documentary series, created by the Discovery Network, is pretty much the most stunning visual imagery of animals in their natural habitat ever made. And if you're more of the old-school type, check out *Microcosmos* which is a documentary about all bugs, big and small, set to an incredible soundtrack.

VISIT

www.nature.org
www.panda.org
www.oceanconservancy.org
www.polarbearsos.org

WATCH

The Discovery Channel's series *Planet Earth*. Watch it in HD if you can to blow your mind!
The documentary film *Microcosmos* (1996) by Claude Nuridsany and Marie Pérennou

139. Green Your School or Workplace

Are you sick of your company's Dunder Mifflin approach to paper products? Tired of using plastic cups every time you go to gossip at the water cooler? Drowning in a sea of harsh lighting while you slave away in your cubicle? Sounds like you have a permanent case of the Mondays when it comes to your job's unfriendly environmental practices. And we think now it's time to do something about it. Get a few of your environmentally focused friends together and set up a meeting to talk to your boss about the eco-friendly changes you'd like to see happen, most of which will probably save the company money in the long run, not to mention a promised return of good karma. Remember, money talks in big business, so if there's any way to help their bottom line then there's a better chance they'll listen.

Here are some tips to get you started:

- Turn off those desk lamps when you're not slaving away at those TPS reports. Duh. If it's what you do at home, you should do it at your cubicle too.
- Put your computer to sleep. And by sleep, we mean *off*. Don't waste precious energy on those slideshows of your pictures from your office party at T.G.I. Friday's.
- Put the kibosh on printing. Unless you absolutely have to, it's time to end those interoffice memos. Send an e-mail; it's just as effective.
- Bring a mug to work. We all know the water cooler is pretty much the go-to place, especially when an awesome episode of *Dancing with the Stars* happens the night before, so we also know how many times that means you're using a new cup. Stop the mad-

ness! And bring your own. And if your company is still using Styrofoam, tell them to get thee out of the '80s, and find a way to help them make the conversion to recycled paper cups.

- Carpool! What a better way to catch up on that office gossip than to share a ride with some of your fellow coworkers?

And if you need help making that argument to your bosses that the time is now for the office to go green, check out these invaluable resources where they have tons of tips to help get your office on the green track.

 **VISIT**

www.treehugger.com
www.planetgreen.discovery.com
www.greenopia.com/USA

140. Save the Forests and Plant a Tree

Do you like to print out your e-mails and documents at work rather than just read them on your computer? If so, then in the immortal words of Donald Trump, "You're fired."

You see, we like our trees. A lot. And not to get all emo on you guys, but it makes us really sad when we hear about how all the world's forests are getting wiped out. Yeah, we know, we need the lumber for "progress" to take place, yada yada yada. Well, there's progress and then there's responsible progress. We'd prefer the latter. That means taking into account the survival of the world's plant and animal species over corporate profits. The rainforests are home to over an estimated 50 percent of all plant and animal species on earth, some of which are still being discovered, and we're still learning how much of a huge role they play in the global ecosystem. Studies show that forests help create the necessary balance of gases in our atmosphere, and deforestation is a major factor in global warming. We're not hard-core tree huggers here, but c'mon, we'd rather be able to breathe than have better toilet paper. Good thing there are superheroes out there that are fighting the good fight. Like Wangari Maathai. Don't know her? Well, you should. This Kenyan woman has helped plant 40 million trees in Africa. Not only are her efforts helping to save the planet, but they also garnered her a Nobel Peace Prize in 2004. Rock on, lady! Even British royalty, Prince Charles the Prince of Wales himself, is championing this cause through his Rainforest SOS campaign. So how about it? Plant a tree in your neighborhood or local park today, and check out these organizations to see what else you can do. Happy planting, people!

VISIT

www.arborday.org
www.greenbeltmovement.org
www.rainforestsos.org
www.greenpeace.org

READ

The Lorax by Dr. Seuss

WATCH

The film *Medicine Man* (1992) starring Sean Connery

141–150. Live by the 10 Green Commandments

These days, we're pretty much surrounded by messages telling us to go green. And for the most part we know there are a few basic things that we should be doing every day. No questions asked. So we've decided to create a list of 10 Green Commandments. Live by it, people, the world will thank you.

141. Thou shall not use plastic bags.

142. Thou shall walk, ride a bike, or use public transportation whenever possible.

143. Thou shall not use regular lightbulbs over florescent ones.

144. Thou shall not waste water. (For general tips on how to conserve water, visit wateruseitwisely.com.)

145. Honor thy local farmer.

146. Thou shall unplug appliances when not in use.

147. Thou shall pay bills online.

148. Thou shall recycle everything possible. (Need help unloading that junk? Check out freecycle.org, a reverse eBay for stuff you no longer want.)

149. Thou shall turn off the light when leaving a room.

150. Thou shall only buy what thee needs.

Want to meet others who share your vow to honor the 10 Green Commandments? Want to get a new job helping Mother Earth? Check out **greendrinks.org** where every month around the globe, people who work in the environmental field meet up, have a few drinks, and talk green. It's a great place to network and meet people who may inspire you to make even more changes in your soon-to-be sustainable life.

VISIT

www.greendrinks.org
www.freecycle.org
www.wateruseitwisely.com
www.simplesteps.org

 WATCH

The documentary film *An Inconvenient Truth* (2006) by Al Gore

FINAL THOUGHTS

"We know the battle ahead will be long, but always remember that no matter what obstacles stand in our way, nothing can withstand the power of millions of voices calling for change."
—President Barack Obama (January 8, 2008)

Well, guys, that's it. You made it through, and we really hope we planted some seeds in your head along the way that you'll take to heart. Making a difference is never easy; in fact it's usually very hard. Our world is one complicated and hectic place, and there are plenty of things that could use some fixing. But at the same time, we should never forget what an incredible time we are living in, where we really do have the power to change things for the better. This is truly one of the most dynamic and empowering ages in history, where technology has given us all the tools we need to reach out and connect with people around the globe in a way that wasn't possible just ten years ago. From your neighbor across the street to your friend across the country to a stranger half a world away, you have the power to change lives for the better if you want to. Don't ever forget that! Look, no one has all the answers to all the problems out there, not even President Obama. But if you're looking to make a change, big or small, for yourself, your country, or your world, find something that you believe in, something that you are passionate about, and get started with learning more. It's a hard thing to get motivated sometimes, but once you start rolling, don't ever let anyone hold you back. You're all rock stars on life's stage, and we can't wait to see what you can do. Rock on people, rock on!

ACKNOWLEDGMENTS

This book could not be possible if not for the wisdom and guidance of the following people: Tony Lyons, Bill Wolfsthal, Alaina Sudeith, Jennifer McCartney, Abigail Gehring, Jeremy Barnicle, Chad Boettcher, Rick Copeland, Elizabeth McKee Gore, Margaret Lydecker, Christy Manso, Laura Nelson, Alicin Reidy Williamson, and everyone that took the time to fill out our not-so-short survey for us! Thank you!

A special shout-out and thanks to all my friends for their support, advice, inspiration, and ideas during this process, especially my tireless assistant Tom, and my family Jon, Shanthi, Jacob, and Mom and Dad.

—Jayan

Extra special thanks to Brendan for being my source of never ending support and inspiration. I love you more than this *wird* can say.

—Melissa

Thank you so much to everyone that helped us out and offered their encouragement along the way. We couldn't have done it without you.

ABOUT THE AUTHORS

Jayan Kalathil

Jayan Kalathil is a communications and marketing professional with extensive experience in the nonprofit, television, and entertainment industries. Throughout his career, he has worked on a variety of issues including arts advocacy, global health, disaster relief, substance abuse treatment, autism awareness, and human rights. When he's not busy trying to save (and travel) the world, he's an avid pop culture enthusiast and television and movie junkie.

Jayan earned his BA in history from the University of California Santa Barbara, and his MBA from Fordham University. A California native, he currently resides in New York City.

Melissa Bolton-Klinger

Melissa Bolton-Klinger is a creative one-woman-band who has written and directed award-winning public service announcements and commercials for the likes of VH1, MTV, G4, the Partnership for a Drug-Free America, and the Global Fund. When she's not using her creativity to make the world a better place, she's trying to discover the antidote for kryptonite. Melissa lives in Brooklyn with her husband and is currently working on her first feature film. To see more of her work, or to get in touch, visit her online at **unicornfactory.com.**